COLOR
ME HOLY

HOLY GOD ➤ HOLY PEOPLE

HUBERT P. HARRIMAN
&
BARRY L. CALLEN

ALDERSGATE
PRESS

COLOR ME HOLY

By Hubert P. Harriman & Barry L. Callen

2nd Edition

Copyright © 2013 Hubert P. Harriman & Barry L. Callen

ALDERSGATE **PRESS**
THE PUBLICATIONS ARM OF

WESLEYAN **HOLINESS** CONSORTIUM

HolinessandUnity.org

In Collaboration with

LAMP POST inc.
www.lamppostpublishers.com
Spring Valley, CA

Printed in the United States of America

Soft Cover ISBN 13:	978-1-60039-303-7
ebook ISBN-13:	978-1-60039-976-3

Library of Congress Control Number: 2014957348

CONTENTS

Holiness....Origin

The Divine Nature

Chapter 1

Flashes of Lightning

God is a God of color and none of it should be lost in his creation. The divine color is never more brilliant and intense than when seen in his holiness. The divine intent is to paint humble believers with this very holiness. There is to be nothing dull or drab about the Christian life. Believers are to be sanctified by being made intensely alive with the very splendor of God. God's true na-ture and highest intention for believers is that they be bathed in the hues of holiness. Christians must not settle for any lesser way.

First thing first. Everything in Christian theology and in the Christian life remains unclear and potentially distorted until the question of God's nature is answered.[1] We limited humans tend to shape our own reality. Reality becomes not what *is* but who *we are*. We view God through our own experience and colored glasses. Whatever our color, our agenda, our perspective, our prejudices, so is God--at least in our eyes and minds. What we think it means to be "spiritual," for instance, depends on our understanding of who the Spirit is and how the Spirit works.

Problems come from more than our frail understandings. Too often we think and act as though our religious quest is about us, our needs, fulfillment, and happiness. This is so wrong. Might much of our "church hopping" be little more than spoiled God-seekers looking for the kind of God that suits personal preferences? Are we trying to transform God rather than allowing ourselves to face transformation? For Christians, our goal should be finding, knowing, following, and *being transformed* by the true God. Our quest should be learning about God's true identity and then experiencing a gracious change into God's holy likeness.

The sad fact is, however, that "not everyone who gets interested in the Bible and even gets excited about the Bible wants to get involved with God."[2] Some concerned Christians knew a very successful eye surgeon and spoke to a blind man about their desire to get him to this doctor, even offering to cover all expenses. The blind man thought about it for a moment then asked, "If I am able to see, will I have to work?" "Yes" was the reply, "you will be able to work like anybody else." Then the blind man said, "If in seeing I have to work, I don't want to see."

This kind of response shocks most of us, but sadly it is what many are doing spiritually: "If, in seeing, I will have to think and act like Jesus, I don't want to see." Even so, knowing and becoming properly related to and transformed by the true God is what the Bible is all about. The color of the great Artist is to become our color. God's beautiful holiness is to be reflected in God's people. Our prayer should be, whatever the cost, color me holy! Once colored with reflections of God's nature, let me work from within that holiness toward the transformation of the people and world around me.

What is the persistent problem? It is our tendency to substitute for the Sovereign God a new Holy Trinity. The Father, Son, and Holy Spirit are replaced in our thinking by an individualized personal trinity of "My Holy Wants, My Holy Needs, and my Holy Feelings."[3] Like spoiled children in a store who are allowed to grab what suits their fancy, we expect God to cater to our desires because "God is love" and what loving parent would not give a child what he or she wants? This breakdown of proper focus, this doctrinal discoloration has colossal consequences. All of a sudden, I am the Creator. God is painted to look like me. My hope is for me to be *my* best self, not God's true and holy reflection in this world through a grace-changed life.

How easy it is to create a "god" in our own image and then use our believing for our own benefit. We have seen people with white skin be offended at encountering a representation of Jesus with black skin. Some people are so committed to the national flag they proudly wave that people of other lands are seriously undervalued, even abused with a good conscience. We paint God with our own brushes and then accept the result as the true color portrait of the divine and the right paths for our lives. The fact is that, when it comes to theology, "where doctrinal differences exist among Christians, it is ultimately the conception of God which is at stake."[4] Our understanding of God tints our thoughts, goals, and actions with true or false colors. How we need the discipline of biblical revelation, especially as read through the person of Jesus!

In these pages, then, we are particularly concerned about understanding properly the nature of God. We believe Jesus to be the very image of God among us, even the actual presence (incarnation) of God in our world. He has come for our understanding and salvation (Col. 1:15). We gain our understanding of Jesus and our hope of salvation through the biblical revelation that focuses on the person of Jesus and relies on the ongoing interpretive work of Christ's Spirit among us. The heart of Jesus is the heart of God. The tints of his thinking and the hues of his actions are those of the Father who is in heaven—and wants to be in us.

The heart of Christian faith is accepting one central claim. Knowing Jesus is to know and become properly related to the very heart of God. The heart of a holy life involves the right relating and abiding. As Jesus points out, we are to abide in him as he abides in the Father (Jn. 15). We are called to join Jesus and, somehow and to some extent, actually participate in the holy life of God, to be colored by the divine colors. As we realize this amazing possibility and accept this gracious invitation, we become holy. In brief, holiness is finding oneness with the true God. Faith, then, becomes wonder-full, vital, colorful, life-changing, even world-changing. Holiness is religion on steroids; it is faith in high definition. It is the answered cry to our prayer, "Color me holy!"

God's True Colors

This book first poses and then seeks to answer the core question. What color is God? What does true holiness look like? We are not looking for shadows of ourselves, but for reflections of God's very being and heart. Our goal goes beyond knowing the true identity of God. It includes becoming and enacting the implications of such knowledge.

To find the answers, we must look through the Spirit's eyes toward Jesus, who then shows us the Father. To see Jesus clearly is actually to see the Father who sent him (Jn. 6:46). God now stands Self-revealed so that we can proclaim with confidence the good news of the divine holiness, the loving nature of God (Acts 17:23). As potential children of the divine, we come to realize that we too are to be holy and loving, grateful and faithful reflections of the divine in this world.

To gain some sense of the true color of God, consider this dramatic scene. God is sitting on the heavenly throne and looking like jasper, a beautifully polished red gemstone. Around the throne is the gorgeous green of an emerald, a rainbow that dazzles the eye, and twenty-four smaller thrones. They are filled by elders dressed in white robes and wearing golden crowns. Coming from the central throne are flashes of bright lightning and the blazing yellow light of burning torches. In front of this throne is a sea of glass glistening like crystal. Four living creatures cap this colorful scene by constantly singing, "Holy, holy, holy, the Lord God the Almighty who was and is and is to come" (Rev. 4:8).

God is surrounded by color. But what color is God? The divine color, beyond human description, is holy love. The Lamb who was slaughtered is also present, making clear that God both radiates and actually is such stunning love. God is at once the green of creation, the white of purity, and the red of redemption. God is the rainbow of sovereign, loving grace. Good Christian theology and proper Christian living are to focus on the biblically-revealed God with whom we can fall in love and from whom eternal life now flows our way. God is

> *As potential children of the divine, we come to realize that we too are to be holy and a loving, grateful, and faithful reflection of God in this world.*

beautiful and supremely lovable, the Trinitarian God who is "not static or standoffish but a loving relationality and sheer liveliness. . .the shining radiance of love."[5]

John Wesley once said that God works "strongly and sweetly." The divine color, then, is a strong and striking red—the potential of exercising sheer power and the streaming blood of real redemption. However, the natural outflow of the divine heart, the preferred manner of God's working is not the glare of coercive power. Instead, it involves delicate pastels, the soft yellows and gentle greens, the sweetness of sacrificial love. When viewed through Spirit-assisted eyes that are looking toward God through Jesus by the Spirit, always under the control of biblical revelation, God's primary color becomes clear. It is a holy brilliance, a rainbow dominated with the hues of holy love (1 Jn. 4:8; Eph. 3:17-18).[6]

In the Bible, "glory" refers to the majesty and shining splendor of God made evident in God's mighty works in the history of the creation. This historical evidence of God's footprints in our world is what humans can manage to see and understand. We gain understanding of God's very nature and will by observing God's presence and activities. We are told that the Son radiates God's glory (Heb. 1:3). God is the Father of glory (Eph. 1:7) and Jesus Christ is the Lord of glory (1 Cor. 2:8; 2 Cor. 4:4). The glory of God that dwells in light unapproachable once blazed about the shepherds when Christ's birth was announced. Later, the disciples of this miracle baby saw God's glory in the earthly life of this Jesus (Jn. 1:14)—crucified and then resurrected!

On one occasion, human sight was completely overwhelming. Peter, James, and John saw Jesus "transfigured." His face "shone like the sun, and his clothes became dazzling white" (Matt. 17:2). It is in the face of Jesus Christ that the light of the knowledge of the glory of God shines into our minds and hearts with enlightening and creative power (2 Cor. 4:6). The colors include a burst of yellow and a blanket of white—eternal light filled with unmingled purity, a glimpse of divine holiness, our path to eternal life.

The Old Testament sets the stage for God's full revelation in Jesus. Its theological base comes down to this. There is only one true God, and this God is actively and lovingly seeking the well being of all creation. For all those who see the bright colors of this beautiful picture and yield to its gentle grace and transforming power, such foundational biblical teaching leads naturally to Jesus Christ and our walking with him in the way of God's holiness.[7] As God is, by God's grace, so can and shall we be!

Reversing the Trend

Recent generations of "holiness" Christian believers have rejoiced in this grace-covered goodness of God and what it can do to transform, re-color humble sinners. They have sought to receive the transforming grace of God and shine *from* his glory and *for* his glory into this dark world. In the process, and in the midst of dramatically changing times and cultures, they have been persecuted on occasion, often have been misunderstood, and sometimes have wandered down blind alleys of their own unfortunate choices. They have sought to think, teach, and live out the divine holiness in their limited ways, and many of them have become frustrated and discouraged. They have given up, defaulted, ceased "going on to perfection."

So many believers have never considered or have abandoned the quest for the highest calling of God on their lives. We judge this unacceptable, no matter how understandable it might be in the face of our frail humanness. We hope to help reverse this downward trend in spiritual expectation and hope.

We have seen the upward vision where souls have come alive with true holiness-- not with a holiness of shibboleths, shabbiness, shallowness, not a holiness of sham and empty words only. They do not walk away from dilemmas and questions, but still walk right into the possibilities of holiness. They walk the halls of our churches, our work places, our universities, and our mission fields, lovingly investing their time with hypocrites, their hearts with sinners, their minds with atheists, their lives with the lost and helpless, and they come out with the color of God shining all over them.

These holy ones are not spiritual "stars"; they are simple saints in the purest and most colorful sense of the word. They are the stabilizers in the church. They contradict the naysayers. You hear them singing words by Johnson Oatman, Jr.:

I'm pressing on the upward way, new heights I'm gaining every day,

Still praying as I onward bound, "Lord, plant my feet on higher ground."

Christians too often settle for walking a lower and lesser way. Forgiven of past sin, they become spiritually satisfied and remain immature in their faith. Relieved of past guilt, they become almost passive in their faith questing. They have been evangelized, but not discipled, born but never grown. Going through the motions of respectable religion becomes enough. But the way of Christ intends to raise the eyes of faith upward, to encourage a noticing of the bright orange that is breaking high over the horizon. It is a call for the forgiven to reach toward more than they yet know or have experienced. To be "saved" is the beginning of the faith journey, not the end. As John Wesley once explained:

> *To be "saved" is the beginning of the faith journey, not the end.*

...whoever finds redemption in the blood of Jesus...has then the choice of walking in the higher or the lower path. I believe the Holy Spirit at that time sets before him [the believer] the "more excellent way," and incites him to walk therein;...to aspire after the heights and depths of holiness—after the entire image of God.[8]

Believers mature as they reach toward the fresh colors of higher ground in the early morning sunshine (Son-shine) of the walk of faith. Forgiveness is the key beginning, yes, but it is only to be the beginning. There yet is the bright new day of God's "most excellent way" (1 Cor. 12:31). The holy God always has holiness in mind, even for us fallen and frail humans.

Therefore, this book seeks to do at least three things to reverse the negative trend of settling for spiritual immaturity, of walking only the lower way, of being satisfied with the forgiveness of past sin, basic and wonderful as that is. It seeks (1) to recover the central biblical call to holiness, (2) to understand some wrong turns that have and still can spoil the upward call, and (3) to encourage today's Christian believers and congregations to embrace the full biblical provision for personal, church, and world transformation. This transformation is the Christian holiness that is to be recovered, reclaimed, re-experienced, and beautifully reflected, all to the glory of God. It is a colorful story that can lead to a bright future for the people of God.

Lightning still flashes around the throne of God. Its bright color and electric power, its gentle shades and loving kindness, its rolling thunder and overwhelming presence combine to give us a glimpse of the true God. The Holy One, quite apart from us, nonetheless reaches our way in holy love as the Great Artist who wishes to color us holy.

Notes

[1] See Allan Coppedge, *Portraits of God: A Biblical Theology of Holiness* (InterVarsity Press, 2001).

[2] Eugene H. Peterson, *Eat This Book* (William B. Eerdman's Publishing Company, Grand Rapids, Michigan/Cambridge, U.K., 2006), 30.

[3] Ibid, 31.

[4] Geoffrey Wainwright, *Doxology: The Praise of God in Worhsip, Doctrine, and Life* (London: Epworth Press, 1980), 287.

[5] Clark H. Pinnock, *Flame of Love: A Theology of the Holy Spirit* (1996), as quoted by Barry L. Callen, *Discerning the Divine: God in Christian Theology* (Louisville: Westminster John Knox Press, 2004), 19.

[6] See the systematic theology of Barry L. Callen that is built around this concept of God. It is entitled *God as Loving Grace* (Evangel Publishing House, 1996).

[7] See this detailed in Barry L. Callen, *Beneath the Surface: Reclaiming the Old Testament for Today's Christian* (Lexington, KY: Emeth Press, 2012). Holiness is a fundamental truth stream that flows throughout the entire Bible.

[8] John Wesley explained this in his sermon titled "The More Excellent Way".

Holiness?.... Of Course

Biblical Revelation

Chapter 2

The Glow of Biblical Beauty

"God himself put it this way: 'I'll live in them, move into them; I'll be their God and they'll be my people.... I'll be a Father to you; you'll be sons and daughters to me. With promises like this to pull us on, let us make a clean break with everything that defiles or distracts us, both within and without. Let us make our entire lives fit and holy temples for the worship of God" (2 Cor. 6:16-18; 7:1, MSG). The Bible glows with the beauty of such a high call-ing.

One American company makes a point of excluding the obvious in its public statements about itself. Some organizational values are considered so basic by Chick-fil-a that there is no need to point them out. They are what some would call "givens." For instance, the expectations of food quality and employee integrity are just to be assumed. Likewise, when we talk about holiness as presented in the Bible and expected in the Christian life, we ought to say, "Holiness? Of course! That's a given!" It glows from the pages of Scripture like the northern lights shine and dance in some night skies. It may be unusual in our experience and not possible at our own initiative, but it still is a biblical given!

Whether from the Old or New Testament, holiness splashes out of the pages of the Bible like a pitcher overflowing with cool, pure, sweet grape juice—wonderful to the taste and so healthy for the spiritual body. William Coker, while teaching at Asbury University, masterfully unpacked this great Bible theme of holiness in one of his classes. He introduced wave upon wave of Scripture references. It was all to make one central point: "You have to accept that the Christian message is one of holiness. You cannot throw it out." It is a given. It is far too prominent to miss and much too important to ignore.

Color is Everywhere!

Scientists tell us that color is deeply embedded in how we perceive the world. The Bible reports that God exploded on the world scene with startling splendor and beauty! In the same way, we contend that color is deeply embedded in how we perceive God. God explodes on the human heart with his glorious beauty! As God began to manifest himself to the children of Israel, the tabernacle became central to the beauty of his presence among them. Concerning all that had to do with this tabernacle, from the building itself to the items involved and the priests who served, we find an amazing display of color. As described in the book of Exodus, it dazzles with the brilliant and sparkling colors of gold, silver, bronze, onyx, blue, purple, scarlet, ruby, topaz, emerald, turquoise, sapphire, diamond, jacinth, agate, amethyst, beryl, and jasper. God is a God of color and, by his presence in us, wants that same color radiating out of our own lives.

I (Hubert) was born and raised in Bolivia, a country very diverse geographically and culturally. The majestic Andean mountains, with sharp peaks and high plains, proclaim their glory and beauty on the west side of the country. On the east are the lush, dense jungles of the lowlands and the vast grasslands that have their own special allure. Whether looking at the land or culture, a wide array of color defines it all. Full, clear, vibrant, bright, living, multiple colors fill the eyes like the sound of Niagara Falls thunders on the ears. From the full skirts of the Quechua women to the full bloom of the tropical paradise, Bolivia is alive with color.

I grew up in the lowlands of Bolivia where my parents were missionaries, with many of those years spent in the vast, thick jungles that stretch down from the Amazon Basin of Brazil into the northeastern territory of Bolivia. The most amazing displays of color dominated my early life like the sights and sounds of fireworks on holidays. There were tropical birds, animals, fish, trees, plants, flowers, and insects. What always captured my attention was the intricately and many-faceted color of the butterflies, especially when the butterflies crowded together on something that was moist. It was pure beauty with wings! Interestingly, the greatest display of butterfly glory appeared when they came together on some mundane object like a fresh dropping of cow dung. That picture always fascinated me.

God also seems to display glorious divine colors in the most inglorious settings, like settling on the mass of sinful people. This is what our glorious God delights in doing—touching wayward humans with divine grace and glory, bringing fresh color and life to places of darkness and death. There is nothing so amazing as God being willing to address lovingly a humanity so given to sin, so dung-laden, so depraved and deformed, and so opposed to God because of sin (Rom. 8:7). The glory of divine grace shines brightly when we see God wanting to impart his beauty to the now ugly, restoring the fallen and igniting a blaze of beauty. While we were yet sinners, God...!

Three times in Scripture we are exhorted to "worship the Lord in holy splendor" (1 Chron. 16:29 and Psalms 29:2 and 96:9). Some versions translate this as "worship the Lord in holy array." We can appreciate both translations because together they capture the color of God

> *The glory of divine grace shines brightly when we see God wanting to impart his beauty to the now ugly, restoring the fallen and igniting a blaze of beauty.*

transferred to the worshipper. They come together in the pure color, beauty, and delight of holiness. Unfortunately, somewhere along the line many of us have lost the luster of the word "holiness," even cleaning it out of our language closets and recycling it at a second-hand religious store with the attitude that it might do someone some good, but I won't be wearing it anymore.

For much too long now, holiness has been seen like some black-and-white TV sitting in a dingy corner of the house. This TV does not work very well and has a pitiful antenna that cannot get much of a signal—if any signal at all depending on the weather and exact direction it is pointed. This kind of holiness should have been dumped in the trash long ago. We must move the subject of holiness from this fuzzy, dull, colorless screen to something more like high-definition television. Here we have a resolution substantially higher than what has been the usual.

Christians need to rediscover the beauty of holiness--the brilliant, splendorous, glorious, delightful, restorative color of God. Only then will we know the sheer joy of having it poured out on us like rain on a dry and thirsty land, like the flowing of rivers of living water. When we do know, says the ancient prophet, "the desert shall rejoice and blossom like the crocus" (Is. 35:1). The crocus is related to the iris and has brightly colored flowers. Such is God. God is holy, but not dull! God exists in living color and wants to paint this color into our lives. Like the rainbow God put in the sky, divine holiness breaks through the darkness of this world with a beautiful array of coordinated colors for us to absorb and reflect. Says the prophet Ezekiel, "This was the appearance of the likeness of the glory of the Lord.... Like the bow in a cloud on a rainy day, such was the appearance of the splendor all around" (1:28).

We must be cautious and keep our thinking balanced. There surely is this bright side of God. It is not that God has a dark side, at least not in the sense of hidden evil. Even so, we have tended to paint many of our assumptions about God as rather ominous—God as austere, stern, solemn and forbidding. Because of this, we often approach anything that has to do with God as necessarily involving suffering, sacrifice, and solemnity. Although these qualities have their vital place in the Christian walk, God wants to wrap even these in the joyous beauty of his loving and lovely holiness.

This divine holiness unfolds with brightness, beauty, joy, gladness, and delight. It fills the heart with joy and song no matter what the immediate circumstances. It was this and only this that could cause the early disciples of Jesus to "consider it all joy" when they encountered various trials (James 1:2). They could embrace suffering as a kind of glory (Philippians 3:10) and even sing in the darkness (Acts 16:25). "Joy to the World" should be more than a popular Christmas carol—it is the Christian's theme song!

In the first chapter we spoke of the beauty of the glorious color that shines out of God's holiness—that of pure love. The colors that radiate from the heart of God are always pure. In order for color to be pure, it must be without contaminates. Such is the color of God, and such is the color that God wants to paint into our lives. John speaks of this color as something as pure as "perfect love" (1 Jn. 4:18)—a love that is fully and always nothing but itself. We should expect no less as God paints with a holy brush on the canvas of our lives.

This holy love, by its very nature, is not individualistic in nature—where it's all about me, my holiness or my purity for my own good. Holiness turns outward, not inward. Holy love is anything but self-focused. It releases us from the narcissism that plagues our world, causing us to "look not to [our] own interests, but to the interests of others" (Phil. 2:4). This is a deep work of God that gets our eyes off ourselves and causes us to think along the line of what the Apostle Paul wrote, "Do nothing from selfish ambition or conceit, but in humility regard others as better than yourselves" (Phil. 2:3). This outward focus takes us out of our "safe" world and places us in the thick of the world with all of its social injustices like bigotry, racism, classism, and other unholy practices. True holiness champions the "and," by "loving the Lord your God with all your heart, soul, mind and strength" *and* "loving your neighbor as yourself."

But stop for a moment. Already the gnawing fingers of doubt begin to squeeze our hopes nearly to death. We wonder if we are setting the bar too high. We dare not construct a fantasy that would do more harm than good, discouraging sincere souls. Are we not surrounded by an ominous cloud of failures? Should we be calling Christians to something that might cause them to live under more condemnation? It is tempting in the face of such negatives to leave the subject of holiness unaddressed. But we cannot, not if we are true to God's Word. Scripture explodes with the color of holiness that is expected and has been experienced. We are not discouraged because holiness is not our idea but God's—it is God's heart and stated intention for us, and it does not rest on our ability but on God's ability and promises.

We feel in our hearts that same stirring that Peter and John felt when they said, "we cannot keep from speaking about what we have seen and heard" (Acts 4:20). Listen to the witness of the Word:

When the Scripture declares, "You shall be holy, for I am holy" (1 Pet. 1:16), that is a promise of divine re-coloring.

When the Scripture declares, "A new heart I will give you, and a new spirit I will put within you; and I will remove from your body the heart of stone and give you a heart of flesh" (Ez. 36:26), that is a promise of divine re-coloring.

When the Scripture declares, "He will baptize you with the Holy Spirit and fire" (Mt. 3:11), that is a promise of divine re-coloring.

When the Scripture declares that God "chose us in Christ before the foundation of the world to be holy and blameless before him in love" (Eph. 1:4), that is a promise of divine re-coloring.

Simon Peter captured the incredible promise of our knowing this divine color entering our drab lives. Who better to speak of this than a man who had failed as miserably as Peter. Sometimes you find color in the most unexpected places. Years later, after experiencing the free and full brush of God splashing the color of God on the canvas of his heart, Peter exclaimed, "His divine power has given us everything needed for life and godliness, through the knowledge of him who called us by his own glory and goodness. Thus he has given us, through these things, his precious and very great promises, so that through them you may escape from the corruption that is in the world because of lust, and may become participants of the divine nature" (2 Pet. 1:3-4).

This marvelous testimony did not come from some smooth, well-groomed, proper person schooled in fancy religious words. This was a wind-blown, sun-burned, temperamental fisherman who always spoke strongly and honestly. He had come to know that God's divine power "has given us everything needed for life and godliness!" Peter had come to know this God who makes huge promises about a sharing of his holy nature. God wants to color us, even the Peters of this world, in shades of loving kindness.

> *God wants to color us, even the Peters of this world, in shades of loving kindness.*

Peter may have been "un-learned" in some people's estimation, but he was not ignorant of the Scriptures. He knew the Torah, the Psalms, and the words of the prophets. The problem was that, like most Jews in his time, Peter could not see the whole of God's revelation. But one day, by the goodness of God, it came together for Peter. He saw these "precious and very great promises," both in their source and scope. Later, he would report about Cornelius, the Gentile centurion who had the same experience. Peter's conclusion? "God, who knows the human heart, testified to them by giving them the Holy Spirit, just as he did to us; and in cleansing their hearts by faith he has made no distinction between them and us" (Acts 15:8-9). The colors of God's holiness that had brightened Peter's life could touch anybody's life, whether Jew or Gentile--even yours and mine.

The amazing beauty of this color displayed in Peter's life would plunge him into a world he had sought to avoid—the world of the "unclean" (Acts 10). This is where the rubber meets the road, where holiness brings its color into the most unexpected places. World Gospel Mission has as a core value a "wholistic approach." This is a deliberate intent "to touch and transform lives, communities and nations" at the deepest level of its deepest needs, whether physical or spiritual, actively praying and participating in the heart of the Lord's Prayer: "Your kingdom come. Your will be done, on earth as it is in heaven" (Matt. 6:10). This approach to ministry will not avoid the sometimes necessary turning over of the tables of the moneychangers in the temple with a holy purpose to make right what is wrong. A holiness without a holy zeal for the wholeness of God's creation is not holiness with complete integrity. God transforms his people so that they might be instruments of wholistic transformation in this desperate world.

After his resurrection, Jesus came alongside two men walking on the road to Emmaus. Like Peter, they knew Scripture like pieces of a puzzle, colorful pieces scattered on a table, with some locked together, some upside down, and some on the floor or still in the box. God wanted them and us to see and enjoy the *whole picture* once put together in the life, death, and resurrection of Jesus. It is a picture of the holiness of divine love originating in God, hanging on the cross of Jesus, bursting from the tomb, and intended to be seen lived out in God's participating people!

And where do we find the entire picture, the whole and holy picture? We can turn for guidance to the cantata of Joseph M. Martin called "Colors of Grace." It celebrates musically the Christian Holy Week. He reports this in the cantata's foreword: "From Thursday evening's Passover meal through Friday's dark hours on the cross, the light of Christ continued to illumine the Truth. With intense clarity, the Teacher was showing us by example the greatest lessons of his ministry: service, obedience, humility, and forgiveness. Through Christ, the full spectrum of God's grace is reflected in beautiful hues upon our lives. In the suffering of this Holy Week, *find joy.* In its darkness, *see Light."*

Jesus helped Peter and the men along the road to put it all together. It is wonderful things when we have this happen in our lives. Like a child receiving the help of someone who knows where each piece of the puzzle fits, we get excited because we are finally beginning to see the whole, capture the meaning, know the promise fulfilled. All of a sudden, pieces of scattered colors become one picture of beautifully coordinated color. This happens to those who become sensitive to the voice of God's Spirit opening the Scriptures to their hungry souls. It then is reflected in what some call the "Christian Year," an annual remembering of the life, death, and resurrection of Jesus—the whole of God's saving and transforming message and the lifeblood of the holiness of the church in all ages.

> The Christian Year is a distinctive and colorful way for believers to mark time. It highlights the biblical pattern of essential memories that inspire spiritual growth and joy!

> Royal Blue (Advent) moves to Pure White (Christmas), then on the Black (Lent) which leads to Brilliant Yellow (Easter), followed by the cleansing of Fire Red (Pentecost) and always the Green of growth in the Spirit—all the white while waiting for the additional arrival of the King of Kings and Lord of Lords!

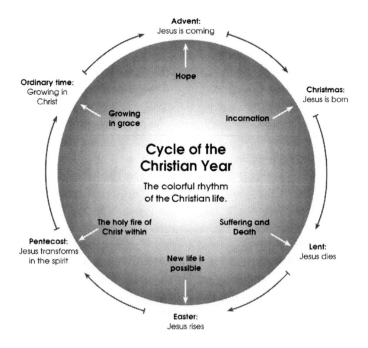

Advent: Jesus is coming

Hope

Ordinary time: Growing in Christ

Christmas: Jesus is born

Growing in grace

Incarnation

Cycle of the Christian Year

The colorful rhythm of the Christian life.

The holy fire of Christ within

Suffering and Death

Pentecost: Jesus transforms in the spirit

Lent: Jesus dies

New life is possible

Easter: Jesus rises

Hungry for Color

A poster in an exercise facility read, "Add color to your life." It was encouraging people to make sure they ate from the five main food groups that are important for each day. Identified were the groups, each by a color—green foods, purple foods, yellow foods, red foods, and orange foods. Often those are the very foods that we struggle getting our children to eat. Parents know that it is important that children acquire a taste for such foods if health and growth are to be assured.

Anyone who has made these foods a part of the daily diet knows they are not only good for you but just plain good. Usually, the problem with those who do not "like" certain healthy foods is less because of the taste of the food and more in the untrained taste of the consumer. Our appetite for fast and junk foods dominates society and is creating huge health problems. Michelle Obama has taken up this problem as a cause in the United States, seeking to reduce the intake, especially among school children, of less healthy foods while trying to get schools to serve healthier foods. It is a noble cause that finally has only one solution, getting children hungry for the colors of health!

> *If we are to be partakers of the divine nature, of the splendor of God's holiness, we must begin with a hungering after God. Holiness defines our proper relationship with God.*

In a similar way, if we are to be partakers of the divine nature, of the splendor of God's holiness, we must begin with a hungering after God. This produces what holiness people used to call "seekers," people whose hearts were set on one thing and who would not be satisfied until they found what their hearts longed for. I (Barry) recently used this "hungry" image in the subtitle of a book.[1] What we now call the Lord's Prayer was intended by Jesus as a way of focusing believers on the central truths of the faith. It begins with a holy hush, a "hallowing" of the very name of God. The whole prayer is for holiness-hungry people—and it ends with a celebration of the unlimited power of God to bring about what is expected and promised.

Dr. Paul Brand tells how seeking and finding happens between a mother and her newborn child. The child has never before eaten with the mouth or even heard of milk. No matter. When hunger becomes real and urgent, the baby somehow knows what to do. The mouth opens, finds the right place on the mother's body, and finds the needed food. The active seeking of the child triggers a response in the mother's body. The mother wants to give and the baby wants to receive—and they both do.[2] This very human process is an apt analogy of the beautiful picture of God's readiness, desire, and ability to respond to our spiritual need.

Infant feeding gives new meaning to Simon Peter's words to the church. "Like newborn infants, long for the pure, spiritual milk, so that by it you may grow into salvation—if indeed you have tasted that the Lord is good" (1 Pet. 2:2-3). In what comes across as an almost desperate plea, God says, "Hear, O my people, while I admonish you; O Israel, if you would but listen to me! There shall be no strange god among you; you shall not bow down to a foreign god. I am the Lord your God, who brought you up out of the land of Egypt. Open your mouth wide and I will fill it" (Ps. 81:8-10). The words "open your mouth wide" call for the hunger to which God willingly responds, especially the hunger for holiness.

Nothing is more frustrating than trying to spoon-feed a toddler who does not want to eat. This process often ends up in a general mess with more food around the mouth and on the highchair than in the child's mouth and stomach. But there is nothing more delightful than feeding a child who, having enjoyed the first bite, readily opens the mouth wide for more. This is pure joy for both parties.

This is what Jesus was responding to when He began to share with the two men on their way to Emmaus. This particular part of the story is fascinating: "Then, beginning with Moses and all the prophets, he interpreted to them the things about himself in all the scriptures" (Lk. 24:27). Can you imagine these moments? Have you ever wondered how many verses Jesus may have quoted? Have you ever wondered what verses he tied together in a fresh way? The same could be asked of Peter's reference to what he calls the "the precious and very great promises God has given us," so that "through them you may participate in the divine nature..." (2 Pet. 1:4).

One thing that becomes evident as we consider the Word of God is that God has refused to leave holiness as some heavenly, otherworldly subject. He brought it right down to earth, touching, filling, and marking very earthy, humble vessels, places and people with his Person—his holy-love color displayed in flesh like ours. God let us touch the divine in Christ—the glory made present with us. The Apostle John said, "And the Word became flesh and lived among us, and we have seen his glory, the glory as of a father's only son, full of grace and truth" (Jn. 1:14). John was so moved in heart by this dramatic fact that he later wrote: "We declare to you what was from the beginning, what we have heard, what we have seen with our eyes, what we have looked at and touched with our hands, concerning the word of life" (1 Jn. 1:1). Theological theory had become experienced reality!

John leaves no doubt. True Christian faith will touch and be touched by, participate in personally and be transformed thoroughly by the very word of life, Jesus Christ the Lord. John Wesley once said it classically: "Dost thou know what religion is? That it is a *participation* of the divine nature; the life of God in the soul of man; Christ formed in the heart;...heaven begun on earth?" Since this is so, what should a humble believer do? "Press forward for the prize of their high calling, even a clean heart, thoroughly renewed after the image of God, in righteousness and true holiness."[3] Recall what Peter wrote: "Conduct yourselves honorably among the Gentiles, so that, though they malign you as evildoers, they may see your honorable deeds and glorify God when he comes to judge" (1 Pet. 2:12).

Many have tried to refute experiential holiness because of what they consider a lack of living proof. The Hindu Mahatma Gandhi is reported to have said that he might well have become a Christian had it not been for the Christians he knew. How sad! Human testimony should be powerful evidence of the great holiness truth, and certainly not a public denial of it. But, finally, it is not proved or disproved by human example, good or bad. What is true is true regardless of how badly some of us might represent it.

Too many Christian doctrines have been formed from human experience and preference rather than from Scriptural authority. The question is not how many living proofs appear to be around us, but *what does Scripture say*? Once Scripture has spoken, that is all we need. Truth stands on the authority of the inspired Word of God, and that is enough. That is the beauty of God's Word; it stands on its own regardless of the frailty of human understanding or living out. We simply need to raise the colors of biblical holiness and live triumphantly out of its promises.

The truth of holiness does not come down on us like some hammer, demanding, difficult, demeaning, and depressing. As Peter wrote, these are "*precious* and very great promises, so that through them you may participate in the divine nature." What are these promises? For the sake of brevity, we will lift up only a few overarching Bible verses. They are representative only. We encourage you to go through the Bible again with a watchful, searching, and hungry heart. You will be overcome with the holy theme, the splendor of holiness that is the provision and expectation of God.

Something needs to be noted, however, as we mine for insights about God's holy beauty found throughout the biblical revelation. We are not searching for isolated "proof" texts to be thrown at a struggling, doubting Thomas. The sheer volume of verses will prove little to the skeptical person. What we are holding up are visual helps for those with hungry hearts. We want such people to see how the many pieces fit together to form a beautiful picture. We want to help seekers find the high road of holiness that takes us home to God.

God spoke to the chosen people, the children of Israel, about this holiness road that leads upward and finally home. It was spoken in relation to their coming release from the long captivity in Babylon. Isaiah announced on God's behalf: "A highway shall be there, and it shall be called the Holy Way; the unclean shall not travel on it, but it shall be for God's people; no traveler, not even fools, shall go astray" (Is. 35:8). It is the biblical way forward, the way so needed by many believers and churches today!

Enjoy the View!

Can you imagine the feeling of those Jewish captives as they finally joined the road that would take them back to their precious homeland? God was letting them know that holiness is not something out there in the distant future. The "Holy Land" is a way by which they—we--can travel in the present moment. Walking that way—God's way—becomes holy as the human nature and will come into conformity with the divine nature and will.

The Holy Land could not be known without the holy way. And land that can be holy is not limited to a small area on the eastern Mediterranean Sea. As one preacher put it when speaking about Moses and the burning bush (Exodus 3), any old bush will do. It is not the place that makes the difference, but the presence of God in that place.

Many seek after holiness as something to strive for but never realize in this life. God, on the other hand, presents it as a way to be known and enjoyed *now* as the only way home to God *then*. There is nothing more inviting, more desirable and wonderful than the road that you know is taking you home. It becomes a part of the vital connection between where you are and where we hope to be.

The realities of my (Hubert) growing up as a missionary kid in Bolivia and the responsibilities of later ministry, especially my current position with World Gospel Mission, have taken me away from home many times. I am a home boy, with all the pleasures the thought of home brings to my memories and emotions. And yet, my lot often has been to "suffer" distance—going off to boarding school, college, speaking engagements, and sometimes to the ends of the earth. The missionary boarding school I attended was in the foothills of the Andean Mountains, far away from where my missionary parents lived and worked. I suffered with homesickness. The redeeming factor was the amazing Pan American Highway extending from Prudhoe Bay, Alaska, in North America, to the lower reaches of South America, and running right by the boarding school. I fell in love with that highway. I felt like it connected me. It was the way home for me, as "the way of holiness" was for the Israelites, and as it should and can be for all of us.

The writer to the Hebrews said, "Pursue...holiness" (12:4). The word pursue has "reference to a course of action to be followed or a pattern of life to be realized, and this with all diligence."[4] This is different from the word "seek" which means you have not yet found what you are looking for. Certainly, if you have not yet found the way, seek for it; but to pursue means that you have found the way and are determined to stay actively on the course. You know that it will get you home. Remember that it is the precious and great promise of God. Enjoy the view. Follow the holiness road all the way home!

Showing the Divine Colors

Holiness is the very nature of God's divine center. Then comes the call to holiness in Scripture. It comes not because it is a mere *concern* of God, but because holiness is the very *character* of God. "Holy is the way God is. To be holy, He does not conform to a standard. He *is that standard.* He is absolutely holy with an infinite, incomprehensible fullness of purity that is incapable of being other than it is. Because He [God] is holy, all His attributes are holy; that is, whatever we think of as belonging to God must be thought of as holy."[5]

God speaks, acts, and expects out of the eternal fountain of the holiness that God is. Holiness as biblically presented is at least all of the following.

Holiness is the central point of God's identification

God was known by various names. They were revealed at various times to various people throughout the Old Testament period. The one name that clearly identified who God is more than any other in the mind of an Israelite was reference to God as "The Holy One of Israel." And this divine name was also to be the name that was to identify them—a holy God intends holy children. This has not changed. This is the name by which God wishes to identify his children today. They are the "saints," the holy ones.

From the high priest of the Old Testament, with the headdress imprinted with the words "Holiness unto the Lord," to the priesthood of the New Testament with its clear understanding that "we are a holy priesthood" (1 Pet. 2:9), God's children are to bear the family name, the name of God, the holy nature of God. For anyone who intends to spend the rest of eternity with God, that name must be honored and assumed. Note the following highlights of biblical teaching.

This is the name by which God is known in the eternities. "And the four living creatures, each of them with six wings, are full of eyes all around and inside. Day and night without ceasing they sing, 'Holy, holy, holy, the Lord God the Almighty, who was and is and is to come'" (Rev. 4:8).

This is the name by which anyone will enter the eternities. It was John who wrote, "Beloved, we are God's children now; what we will be has not yet been revealed. What we do know is this: when he is revealed, we will be like him, for we will see him as he is. And all who have this hope in him purify themselves, just as he is pure" (1 Jn. 3:2-3).

This is the name by which God's children are identified eternally. Here is our eternal ID, if you will. John writes of those who will see God's face, saying, "and his name will be on their foreheads" (Rev. 22:4). Sin is turning one's face away from God. Our sanctification as believers involves turning our full faces back toward God and away from ourselves. Could it be that, when we see God as he is, our faces will bear the divine likeness? His name (his nature—his holiness) will be on our foreheads. Eternity will only engrave more deeply what we by grace already are in this world.

The Holy Trinity (God) who created humans in God's image and likeness wants nothing less than God's image and likeness in us again. Speaking of that eventual time and place, John brings his great book of Revelation to a close with the words, "Let the righteous still do right, and the holy still be holy" (Rev. 22:11). Holiness is the central point of the whole biblical story, right to the last words.

Holiness is the central point of God's exaltation

Historically, the church has championed *Soli Deo Gloria* (Latin phrase for "glory to God alone"), but it also has stumbled with the tendency to glorify church leaders and structures in the face of God. We all appreciate human accomplishments, achievements, abilities, and acts that separate certain people from the norm. Still, when we begin to exalt them, as we do these days with athletes, singers, movie stars, politicians, and royalty, we set ourselves up for divisions, disappointments, and disillusionments.

Anytime we lift someone up, that person likely will let us down, for no human being or human system can continually, and certainly not finally, meet our deepest human needs or God's highest expectations. The church has erred most when it has exalted human beings and human systems most. It is a misplaced trust that takes our eyes off the Lord of Lords and King of Kings. He is the only One who is worthy of our praise, honor, glory, and exaltation. This love affair with human "stars" has cheapened the church's image and damaged the church's authority. The true saint of God stands tallest when kneeling in the greatest humility.

Perhaps this is what happened to Isaiah when he sought a place of prayer (Isa. 6:1). King Uzziah had brought hope for the kingdom of Judah, but he had wasted it on self-exaltation (2 Chron. 26:15). Strength became his pride and pride became his downfall: "But when he had become strong he grew proud, to his destruction. For he was false to the Lord his God, and entered the temple of the Lord to make offering on the altar of incense" (2 Chron. 26:16). Politics had tried to usurp the place and practice of the priests, but the priests did not retreat. Even in Uzziah's furious anger against them (v19), they had the courage to stand up to him. Finally, the Lord struck the king with leprosy and he was excluded from the house of the Lord (2 Chron. 26:21).

When high hopes had been dashed on the rocks of human weakness, Isaiah knew that he needed to seek hope at a higher and more dependable level. Whenever God's people begin to earnestly seek after this higher (holy) level, the cobwebs of wrong thinking and misplaced trust get brushed away. Like a rich, colorful, and priceless oil painting that has been discovered in an old and forsaken storage room, humble prayer rediscovers what was lost. It is in the place of fresh humility and earnest prayer that we again see the unseen and hear the unheard.

Isaiah writes, "In the year that King Uzziah died, I saw the Lord sitting on a throne, high and lofty; and the hem of his robe filled the temple. Seraphs were in attendance above him; each had six wings: with two they covered their faces, and with two they covered their feet, and with two they flew. And one called to another and said: 'Holy, holy, holy is the Lord of hosts; the whole earth is full of his glory'" (Isa. 6:1-3).

Holiness? Of course! This is God's separateness! This is God's otherness! This is God's singular splendor! This is God's beautiful, loving color that both blinds and finally opens eyes! Holiness is the central point of God's exaltation and the only hope of God's people.

Holiness demands a different kind of relationship with God. The "holy, holy, holy is the Lord of hosts" moves one from the thoughtless and shallow claims of much that passes for "praise and worship" these days to a deep sense of the sacredness, wonder, and awe of God's name and presence. This takes the silliness out of our religion and questions many of the "ditties" we promote as sacred songs. Scripture texts like 1 Chronicles 16:28-29 turn empty worship on its head: "Ascribe to the Lord, O families of the peoples, ascribe to the Lord glory and strength. Ascribe to the Lord the glory due his name; bring an offering, and come before him. Worship the Lord in holy splendor." God's holiness demands a different kind of worship, raising it from an infatuation with volume and tempo to true adoration and praise of the divine.

Holiness defines our proper relationship with God. One does not stay very long before the throne of God without recognizing that sin has no place. Isaiah responds by saying, "Woe is me! I am lost, for I am a man of unclean lips, and I live among a people of unclean lips; yet my eyes have seen the King, the Lord of

> *One does not stay very long before the throne of God without recognizing that sin has no place.*

hosts!" (Isa. 6:5). Anyone who has ever been in this holy place knows that there is no remaining there without radical transformation. It brings a cry of the heart—not one of hopelessness, but of fresh hopefulness. It is like a lover declaring unworthiness and yet looking for the smile, the touch, the welcoming hand of the one deeply loved. The hope is for favorable body language from the one loved, anything that indicates acceptance and love returned. At the high throne of divine grace, God's body language is always "Yes!"

Holiness draws us into an intimate relationship with God. Paradoxically, the holiness of God is something both to fear and not to fear. The holiness of God is the drastic difference between God and humans, but it also can be the delightful likeness between God and humans. The holiness of God keeps us from touching the sacred (in the wrong way), but does not keep the sacred from touching us (in the right way). And that is exactly what God did with Isaiah. Listen to his testimony: "Then one of the seraphs flew to me, holding a live coal that had been taken from the altar with a pair of tongs. The seraph touched my mouth with it and said: 'Now that this has touched your lips, your guilt has departed and your sin is blotted out'" (Isa. 6:6-7). The holiness of God begets holiness in humble humans. "O magnify the Lord with me, and let us exalt his name together" (Ps. 34:4).

Holiness is the central point of God's incarnation

God in Christ Jesus demonstrates the beautiful union of holiness and humanity, proving convincingly that our problem is not humanity itself but our sinfulness. God in Jesus removed the partition between us and made it possible for us to actually enter the Holy of Holies. The high priest had stood as the agent of God for the people. Nothing unclean could pass through the curtain. God had a purpose in the coming of Jesus—to get us to the other side of the curtain in this life!

The writer to the Hebrews, captivated and enthralled by this truth, exclaims, "We have this hope, a sure and steadfast anchor of the soul, a hope that enters the inner shrine behind the curtain where Jesus, a forerunner on our behalf, has entered, having become a high priest forever according to the order of Melchizedek" (Heb. 6:19-20). This is why Jesus came—he was the ultimate high priest, the only high priest who could make it possible for us to get into the inner shrine behind the curtain. His incarnation was absolutely essential to make this possible because it would take the power of the cross and the resurrection to make it happen.

The power of the cross

The grand painting of redemption has one element that makes the painting come to life--shadow. Without proper shades, a painting takes on brightness without life. There was a shadow that fell across the world one day, the shadow of the cross, and it brought hope that we could not only be forgiven but transformed. The writer to the Hebrews saw the meaning of this shadow when he said, "Jesus...suffered outside the city gate in order to sanctify [make holy] the people by his own blood" (13:12). The shadow of that cross reached far and wide.

> *It reached back, fulfilling prophecy.* Isaiah prophesied that "he was wounded for our transgressions, crushed for our iniquities; upon him was the punishment that made us whole, and by his bruises we are healed. All we like sheep have gone astray; we have all turned to our own way, and the Lord has laid on him the iniquity of us all" (53:5-6).

> *It reached up, satisfying divine law.* Paul wrote that "the wages of sin is death, but the free gift of God is eternal life in Christ Jesus our Lord" (Rom. 6:23). He also confirmed that "for our sake he [God] made him to be sin who knew no sin, so that in him we might become the righteousness of God" (2 Cor. 5:21).

> *It reached as deep as the stain has gone.* Peter wrote, "He himself bore our sins in his body on the cross, so that, free from sins, we might live for righteousness; by his wounds you have been healed" (1 Pet. 2:24). Paul picks up this same theme: "We know that our old self was crucified with him so that the body of sin might be destroyed, and we might no longer be enslaved to sin" (Rom. 6:6). Thus, Paul could say to Titus that [Jesus] gave himself for us that he might redeem us from all iniquity and purify for himself a people of his own who are zealous for good deeds" (Titus 2:14).

> *It reached out, drawing all of us to God.* Jesus said, "'Very truly, I tell you, unless a grain of wheat falls into the earth and dies, it remains just a single grain; but if it dies, it bears much fruit.... And I, when I am lifted up from the earth, will draw all people to myself.' He said this to indicate the kind of death he was to die" (Jn. 12:24). From the criminal on the cross to the centurion looking on and then to the world all around Him, the shadow of Christ crucified would reach out with a holy healing.

The power of the resurrection

Paul put the possibility of holiness directly in relation to the power of the resurrection: "Therefore we have been buried with him by baptism into death, so that, just as Christ was raised from the dead by the glory of the Father, so we too might walk in newness of life" (Rom. 6:4). Paul voices this same theme by declaring with great emotion, "I want to know Christ and the power of his resurrection" (Phil. 3:10). So should we all.

What significance does the resurrection play in our lives beyond being a major historical anchor of the Christian faith? Could it be that "we talk as if Jesus were alive but then we live as if he were dead? In the resurrection of Christ more is possible that you ever dreamed."[6]

God covered Christ with royal colors as the victor over death, the Lord of life who has proved himself mighty to save to the uttermost.

Holiness, then, is the central point of God's expectation

It cannot be stated strongly or often enough. "But as he who called you is holy, you *also* are to be holy in all your conduct, because it is written, 'Be holy, for I am holy'" (1 Pet. 1:15-16). Holiness is not merely a good idea, an honored church hope. Holiness is the very essence of who God is and what God expects. All of God's dealings with the creation are determined and demonstrated out of this essence. All of our believing and living as followers of Christ is to be determined and demonstrated out of this divine essence seen and shared.

We Christians often speak of the pillars of our faith, pivotal events and beliefs on which our faith is based. Pillars are what hold the structure up. Take any pillar down and the structure can crumble. This is especially true with the pillar of holiness. Holiness is the center pole that holds up the tent of biblical revelation. Take this down and the whole tent comes down. That's a given!

We may have many questions about the pillar of holiness, and many of them will be addressed in the chapters to follow, but do not allow unanswered questions to destroy the pillar. We need not be afraid to ask the questions, but we can ill afford to remove the holiness pillar from our faith's home. God can handle the questions, but we cannot handle the crumbling of this vital truth in our lives and churches. The integrity of our faith depends on it. Holiness is the glowing of biblical beauty.

Notes

[1] Barry L. Callen, *The Prayer of Holiness-Hungry People: A Disciple's Guide to the Lord's Prayer* (Francis Asbury Press, 2011).

[2] Paul Brand, *He Satisfies My Soul* (Discovery House Publishers, 2008).

[3] From John Wesley's sermon "The Righteousness of Faith," and from his Journal, vol. 1, 284. Emphasis added.

[4] H. Orton Wiley, *The Epistle to the Hebrews* (Kansas City, Missouri: Beacon Hill Press, 1959), 395.

[5] A.W. Tozer, *The Knowledge of the Holy* (N.Y.: Harper and Row, 1961), 112-113.

[6] Steve DeNeff, "Living the Resurrection," sermon preached at College Wesleyan Church, Marion, Indiana, April 28, 2013.

Chapter 3

The Many Shades of the Light

The Bible is a long and colorful narrative about a holy God creating perfectly and then seeking to redeem a fallen creation—holiness originally estab-lished and then later re-established over many centuries and at great cost. God originally said, "Let there be light" (Gen. 1:3). Much later there came a life that "was the light of all people" (Jn. 1:4). The biblical story involves the many shadows and shades of this amazing story of holiness created, lost, and regained.

We have made clear that the subject of holiness is central to the entire biblical revelation to us and its expectation of us. The Bible is the story of God calling a people to be "a chosen race, a royal priesthood, *a holy nation*, God's own people, in order that you may proclaim the mighty acts of him who called you out of darkness into his marvelous light (1 Pet. 2:9).

Holy love is the overflowing of God's very nature toward the creation. It is the hope of sinful humans. It is clear biblical teaching. If God is holy, the deepest desire of the divine is that the creation reflects that holiness. Again, the Bible puts it clearly: "For I am the Lord...your God; you shall be holy, for I am holy" (Lev. 11:45). But how? Holiness seems beyond human experience, maybe beyond human possibility. Holiness people over the generations have had difficulty explaining and living out their testimonies (see chapters 4 and 5). The Bible records numerous instances of such frustrations and failures.

Nonetheless, the bright and holy light of God has shone in order that a holy people might emerge and that, through that special people, that special treasure of God, the world may come to know. Holiness is a comprehensive biblical theme. It also is a complex one since "long ago God spoke to our ancestors in *many* and *various* ways by the prophets..." (Heb. 1:1). The light of holiness has many dimensions and shades of the one true light.[1]

I See the Rainbow!

My wife and I (Barry) were sitting in the dining room of a large ship when she announced seeing a stunning sight outside the round window by our table. It had just suddenly appeared and captured her attention. There it was, a truly dramatic rainbow that was vivid, seemed so close, and arched right down into the welcoming water. Wow! Few words were said, just the enlarged eyes of one person after another coming over to look. Temporarily, the wonderful meal set before us was being neglected. Nature (God) was somehow streaming unexpected beauty into our eyes and lives.

The rainbow has always dazzled human eyes. Because it is so unusual and beautiful, and has been difficult to account for scientifically until recent times, attempted explanations of it have been common. They are found in the mythologies of many cultures. Such a dramatic display of color demands some kind of interpretation, probably one bigger than typical life on earth. People have thought that the rainbow must have divine origins and meanings. What are they?

In Greco-Roman mythology, the rainbow was considered a path across the sky made by a messenger (Iris) traveling between earth and heaven. In Chinese mythology, it was considered a slit in the sky sealed by a goddess using stones of five different colors. In the mythology of the Arabian Peninsula, the rainbow was viewed as God's war bow. In the ancient Epic of Gilgamesh, the rainbow was thought to be the jeweled necklace of the Great Mother Ishtar. The Irish leprechaun's secret hiding place for his pot of gold was said to be somewhere at the end of the rainbow. Unfortunately, this mysterious place is impossible to reach because the rainbow is a mobile optical effect that depends in part on the location of the viewer.

In the Bible, the rainbow came to be understood as a reflection of God's promise. It represents a holy and very reassuring message from God, and it was a direct response to Noah's sacrificial offering to the Lord, as we see in Genesis 8:20-21 and 9:13-15: "Then Noah built an altar to the Lord, and took of every clean animal and of every clean bird, and offered burnt offerings on the altar. And when the Lord smelled the pleasing odor, the Lord said in his heart, 'I will never again curse the ground because of humankind, for the inclination of the human heart is evil from youth; nor will I ever again destroy every living creature as I have done.... I have set my bow in the clouds, and it shall be a sign of the covenant between me and the earth. When I bring clouds over the earth and the bow is seen in the clouds, I will remember my covenant that is between me and you and every living creature of all flesh; and the waters shall never again become a flood to destroy all flesh'."

This is the biblical explanation of rainbows, one ending with an astounding declaration of an enduring divine love. Martin Luther said, "If I was God and was treated the way the world has treated God, I would kick the world to pieces." God, on the other hand, having every right to completely annihilate the world, and under no obligation to offer any other remedy, chooses to paint the sky with love and fill the world with hope. Hope glistening in God's skies means that there is a way out of this world's sinful mess. Love says in the beautiful stripes of shining color, "I'll make a way. I'll have patience. I'll shower you with hope. I am holiness throughout eternity and I wish holiness in the creation—and I will open fresh doors to its possibility."

> Hope glistening in God's skies means that there is a way out of this world's sinful mess.

In a very real sense, God was saying to Noah and all of us that, because "the inclination of the human heart is evil from youth" (Gen. 8:21), "I will never again cleanse the earth with flood, but I will cleanse individual hearts with blood—the very blood of my own Son." In other words, what the flood of mass death could not do to bring holiness on the earth, Christ through one death would do to bring holiness in the heart. The divine intent was pictured in Isaiah 53, "he was wounded for our transgressions, crushed for our iniquities...and by his bruises we are healed," and it was promised in Jeremiah 31, "I will put my law within them, and I will write it on their hearts; and I will be their God, and they shall be my people."

This intent and promise were huge. No wonder the smell of Noah's sacrificial offering was a "pleasing aroma" to the Lord. Smells can stir up precious memories, and this was a "memory" of the promise of something major yet to come. In this memorable moment that stretched forward to the sacrifice of Jesus, the Son, God reacted by throwing a colorful rainbow across the sky as a sign of hope for a world in desperate need of restored holiness. The crucifixion of Jesus would be marked by darkness across the earth; his resurrection would be a flash of new light and life, a new rainbow day for humanity.

In an important sense, the entire Bible is God's written rainbow. It reflects the various dimensions of the loving revelation of God. Its colors fill us with the fullness of the holiness glow—God's by nature and ours by a gift of grace. This is not an optical illusion with a mythical pot of gold impossible to reach. God's colored ribbon of love, if followed with all the heart, will bring any sincere seeker to the sparkling riches of divine grace received and holiness restored. At the base of this divine rainbow are gems such as this world has never seen.

A rainbow is composed of the entire spectrum of the colors of visible light, from the longest wavelength, red, to the shortest, violet. The order of colors in a rainbow is: red, orange, yellow, green, blue, indigo, and violet. Red is at the top edge and violet at the bottom edge, with the other colors in between. Here is the alpha and the omega, the full range of beauty, the complete richness of God's colorful being and creation. Here is the stunning divine promise that inspires the prayer of high-definition, full-colored holiness:

> **Red**—amaze me, God, with the bright essence of
>
> Your being—the top edge where it all begins;
>
> **Orange**—keep me alert, God, to the evil dangers
>
> that linger threateningly on all hands;

Yellow—caution me when anything alien to You seeks to invade my life;

Green—keep me always going on to realize in myself the perfections of Yourself;

Blue—soften my will into gentle submission to Your higher will and way;

Indigo—allow the deep and bright beauty of your holiness to color my life through and through;

Violet—comfort me with the Spirit's quiet assurance that will be my all in all, now and forever. Here is hope in the promise of shared and eternal holiness.

A River in the River

The hope of holiness cuts through Scripture like the Great Rift Valley cuts through northern Syria in southwest Asia and runs clear to central Mozambique and South Africa. This geographical wonder, stretching 3,700 miles as a continuous valley, would go largely unnoticed if not seen in the larger perspective now available from far above. Once you know it is there, you actually see it and cannot help but marvel.

Such is the truth and hope of holiness that runs through Scripture. It is amazing how many people never even notice a dramatic rainbow until someone points it out. And then, there it obviously is in all of its splendor! How could we not see it? To use a common phrase, holiness is the "elephant in the room." It is the river within the river, the sub-text of the whole biblical text. God wants it to be seen and embraced.

When I (Hubert) was just out of college, I flew to Bolivia to join with a younger brother in the fulfillment of the dream of our lives—to follow one of the meandering rivers where I had grown up, taking it to larger rivers, and finally on to the Amazon River and finally to the Atlantic Ocean. We had a small boat for the first part of this venture before boarding larger boats as rivers got bigger. We finally managed to catch a ride on a Bolivian navy boat.

I soon began to notice that the pilots of this boat were "meandering" (or so I thought) on the river, going near one shore and then the other, and sometimes traveling in the middle. Curious about this meandering, I asked one pilot why he was not going right down the middle of the river. He said, *"Hay un rio en el rio"* (There's a river in the river). He meant that we had to follow a deeper stream in the river or we could hit rocks. There is nothing, he explained, more important than realizing the location of the river in the river.

When reading the Bible, it is easy to be driven by private agendas, taking shortcuts down the middle to save time, missing the depths and risking the rocks. There is a safe and pure stream that runs through the whole of Scripture. If we don't see it, we will get caught up in following after things that can sidetrack us from the main thing. There is a holiness river in the wide textual river of the Bible.

The entire Bible is about holiness—granted, violated, restored, and regained by divine grace. This river in the river runs clear through Scripture, bringing it all together in one main theme like the tracks of a train crossing the many national borders of Europe. There is wisdom in affirming the "and" that ties together the parts of many things.[2] This is very true when speaking of the Old *and* New Testaments. A full understanding of biblical holiness involves seeing the strong connection between the teaching of the two biblical counterparts.[3]

Holy Glows in the Bible

Taking this all-Bible view, let us share a series of places and ways that holiness appears throughout the biblical revelation. Be prepared. It glows on nearly every page. It is deep and must be followed with care.

Holiness is seen in the eternal purpose of God

The Apostle Paul announced that God "chose us in Christ before the foundation of the world to be holy and blameless before him in love" (Eph. 1:4). He connected the Old with the New Testaments. The God who said "Let us make humankind in our image, according to our likeness" (Gen. 1:26) had not waved the white flag of defeat. Satan had not won! God refused to settle for some kind of treaty that would divide humans—some for God and some for Satan.

This enduring holy purpose of God is our hope. We are God's creation and God intends nothing less than our full redemption, full regeneration, the full restoration of all hearts to their original status. Like the restorers of marred artifacts of great value, God has taken the brush of patient grace and waged war on evil. The whole letter to the Ephesians rings with this great theme.

For instance, Paul offers a profound prayer for the actualizing of this divine purpose: "For this reason I bow my knees before the Father, from whom every family in heaven and on earth takes its name. I pray that, according to the riches of his glory, he may grant that you may be strengthened in your inner being with power through his Spirit, and that Christ may dwell in your hearts through faith, as you are being rooted and grounded in love. I pray that you may have the power to comprehend, with all the saints, what is the breadth and length and height and depth, and to know the love of Christ that surpasses knowledge, so that you may be filled with all the fullness of God" (Eph. 3:14-19).

One can imagine Paul jumping to his feet in jubilation as he takes in the magnitude of this divine work. He raises his hands high as he tastes the glory of this great victory, shouting, "Now to him who by the power at work within us is able to accomplish abundantly far more than all we can ask or imagine, to him be glory in the church and in Christ Jesus to all generations, forever and ever. Amen" (Eph. 3:20-21).

Paul, stirred by the heart and intention of God, turns to the church and implores believers to claim for themselves all of this divine wonder. He says, "I therefore, the prisoner in the Lord, beg you to lead a life worthy of the calling to which you have been called" (Eph. 4:1). God has raised the divine colors and they are hardly the colors of defeat. They are colors that should allow us to "serve him without fear, in holiness and righteousness before him all our days" (Lk. 1:75). Therefore, "to him be glory in the church and in Christ Jesus to all generations, forever and ever. Amen" (Eph. 3:21). Yes, holiness is the eternal purpose of God.

Holiness is seen in the creativity of God

We are told this in 2 Corinthians 5:17: "So if anyone is in Christ, there is a new creation: everything old has passed away; see, everything has become new!" The "everything" is holiness restored. If there is anything we know about God, it is this. God creates and what is created is "good." Following God's creating of man and woman "in his image, in his likeness," the writer says, "God saw everything that he had made, and indeed, it was *very good*" (Gen. 1:31). God has not changed his intention or lost his touch!

The Apostle Paul uses "new creation" language when speaking of anyone who is in Christ: "For we are His workmanship, created in Christ Jesus for good works, which God prepared beforehand so that we would walk in them" (Eph. 2:10, NASB). The Greek word for "workmanship" is *poiema* from which we get our English word "poem." God is truly a word artist who paints and weaves into our lives the very colors and threads of his heart. There is nothing more beautiful than seeing someone walking in harmony with God's colorful and exciting cadence. On the other hand, we are witnessing today, both in the world and even in the church, the unhappy consequences of those who are out of rhythm with God's master plan. God is constantly creative.

Holiness is seen in the Son of God

The Apostle John ties the New Testament to the Old as he begins his Gospel: "In the beginning was the Word, and the Word was with God, and the Word was God. He was in the beginning with God. All things came into being through him, and without him not one thing came into being. What has come into being in him was life, and the life was the light of all people. The light shines in the darkness, and the darkness did not overcome it…. And the Word became flesh and lived among us, and we have seen his glory, the glory as of a father's only son, full of grace and truth…. No one has ever seen God. It is God the only Son, who is close to the Father's heart, who has made him known" (1:1-18). Note the use of the words describing the color of God in Christ—life, light, and glory. Jesus exudes the brilliant holiness of God—God enfleshed in living color!

The writer to the Hebrews masterfully captures the full beauty of this holiness seen in Jesus, the Son of God. Listen to the sound of writer's brush as he paints the brilliant color of this One who cascades over the falls of time and eternity. Follow the flow of the writer's hand as he begins to fill the canvas with the pure color of divinity, expressing the very meaning of life. Who is Jesus? "And He is the radiance of His [God's] glory and the exact representation of His nature, and upholds all things by the word of His power. When He had made purification of sins, He sat down at the right hand of the Majesty on high" (Heb. 1:3).

Have you ever looked at a painting that just took your breath away? Words could not describe what you felt. Here is that painting. What we lack in words the Bible has supplied in a moving scene. Join in the delight of these voices as they are viewing God in Jesus Christ.

John writes: "Then I looked, and I heard the voice of many angels surrounding the throne and the living creatures and the elders; they numbered myriads of myriads and thousands of thousands, singing with full voice, 'Worthy is the Lamb that was slaughtered to receive power and wealth and wisdom and might and honor and glory and blessing!' Then I heard every creature in heaven and on earth and under the earth and in the sea, and all that is in them, singing, 'To the one seated on the throne and to the Lamb be blessing and honor and glory and might forever and ever!' And the four living creatures said, 'Amen!' And the elders fell down and worshiped" (Rev. 5:11-14).

Yes, amazing! "He [Jesus] is the radiance of His [God's] glory and the exact representation of His nature" (Heb. 1:3). When we ask about the color of God, we must look through the Spirit's eyes toward Jesus. To see him clearly is to see the Father who sent him (Jn. 6:46). Seeing him clearly brings from the mouth only, "Holy, holy, holy, the Lord God the Almighty, who was and is and is to come" (Rev. 4:8). In this great truth, this moving master picture that displays Jesus in the Father and the Father in Jesus, Christianity stakes its very life. With an unshakable conviction, many Christians have given their lives—and found new life. The only appropriate response is—color *me* holy!

Scripture declares both that Jesus is fully God with us for our salvation and that he is fully human, one of us except for our sin. Therein lies the greatest beauty, the ultimate mystery of all. There has been a disparaging of humanity that has taken place in much of Christian thinking. It says that being human is the real problem. In fact, being human is our greatest blessing. God created humanity as the culmination of his work and called it all good. We use our humanity as an excuse for poor behavior and attitudes with the common statement, "I'm only human." Although there is no doubt that sin has affected our humanity in many ways, the real problem is not that we are human, but that we have been impacted deeply by sin and need a restored holiness to again be truly human as originally created.

When Jesus was born to Mary, he became flesh with all that it means to be fully and truly human. In Christ, we have a man, like any of us, affected by sin, but unlike us, not *infected* with sin. The problem with humans is not that we are human, but that we have become sinful. We are God's creation—and each somebody is a special somebody in the eyes of the God. In our purest form, we are a colorful people. God aims to restore our original color, sending Jesus as the perfect picture of what God wants painted again on the canvas of our hearts.

After the morning sermon, a small boy went up to the pastor and posed a question about something that had confused him. "Certainly," said the pastor. To which the boy

> God aims to restore our original color, sending Jesus as the perfect picture of what God wants painted again on the canvas of our hearts.

responded, "You said Jesus was a man." "Yes," said the pastor with a quizzical look. "And you also said Jesus could come into my heart." "Yes," replied the pastor with interest. The boy went on, explaining that he was confused because, "If Jesus is a man and I'm just a little boy, if he comes into my heart, he'll be sticking out all over!" With the wisdom of a man who knew the beauty of the truth, the pastor smiled and said, "Yes, he will! God wants everybody to see him in you." We should sing again with deep fervor these wonderful words:

> Let the beauty of Jesus be seen in me,
>
> All His wonderful passion and purity,
>
> Oh, Thou Spirit Divine, all my nature refine,
>
> 'Til the beauty of Jesus is seen in me.[4]

Again, God delights in who we are as humans, but not in our sinfulness as fallen humans. We see significance of the second part of the great verse, Hebrews 1:3. Not only is the Christ "the reflection of God's glory and the exact imprint of God's very being" but also, before he would take his place "at the right hand of the Majesty on high," he *made purification for sins.*" It was for this that he came. It is in this that we have hope.

Do you see it? It is "the river in the river!" "Therefore Jesus also suffered outside the city gate in order to sanctify the people by his own blood" (Heb. 13:12). "Worthy is the Lamb that was slaughtered to receive power and wealth and wisdom and might and honor and glory and blessing!" (Rev. 5:12). As we navigate down the rivers of our times, we must be careful to stay in the Jesus channel. That is where the deep and holy water always is.

Holiness is seen in the will of God

Nothing is more relevant to our day than the clear language of the Apostle Paul to the church at Thessalonica. It concerns sexual purity: "It is God's will that you should be sanctified: that you should avoid sexual immorality" (1 Thess. 4:3, NIV). Immorality was common in pagan religions. The gods and goddesses often were grossly immoral. Priestesses provided sexual services for men who attended the temples. Such must not be so among Christians. Such activity is offensive to the holy God known in Jesus.

Sexual purity is rooted in the beauty of holiness, liberating one from the perversions of the world, transforming our hearts and minds, bringing them into conformity with the delights of God's nature and plan. The sex life of the Christian can and should be an expression of holiness. God demands the purification of all human affections and the restoration of both men and women to the holy status originally planned for humanity.

Sin, no matter how anyone tries to brightly paint it, always remains dreadfully drab, damaging humanness, degrading and destroying human dignity. It defaces God's master painting and then dares to describe the result as "modern art." From the world's point of view, sin is inevitable and justified with bazaar reasoning that supposedly makes it acceptable. How sad that some Christians fall for this kind of false color.

A respected professor from a well-known Christian university was on his way to a small group meeting where he was to discuss biblical holiness. He met a professing "Christian" student and got in a conversation about where each was going. At the professor's response, the student was skeptical about the possibility of holiness. He unashamedly said, "I plan to sin every weekend when I visit my girlfriend." This kind of thinking does not come from God. It comes from other gods who ask, "Did God really say, 'You must not eat from any tree in the garden?'" (Gen. 3:1, NIV). This ancient doubt about God's standards has clouded the beauty and bountifulness of God's holiness ever since.

From the very beginning, God has presented us with everything that is rich, healthy, and delightful—more than enough to eat and enjoy. God gives everything that is "pleasing to the eye and good for food" (Gen. 2:9, NIV). God cares about beauty and health and protects us with holy resolve from anything that will rob us of either (Gen. 2:17). Holiness is God's will, the greatest desire of the divine heart for a creation now vandalized and disfigured.

> Holiness is God's will, the greatest desire of the divine heart for a creation now vandalized and disfigured by sin.

Leprosy was one of the most dreaded, debilitating, disfiguring, and demoralizing diseases known during the Old and New Testament periods. Those stricken were the "untouchables" of society. One of the more touching stories in the ministry of Jesus is when a leper came and knelt before Him, saying, "Lord, if you are willing, you can make me clean" (Matt. 8:2, NIV). What amazing insight! The leper was appealing to the very desire and design of God. Healing, wholeness, and holiness are indeed what God wants to do!

I (Hubert) remember my oldest daughter as a little girl coming to the church office (which was right next to the parsonage) and saying to the pastor, "Daddy, if you wanted to you'd play with me." Now, what kind of Dad could say "no" to that? What was she doing? She was appealing to my deep interest in her, and I was easily moved by this kind of appeal. Jesus responded to the leper by reaching out his hand and touching him, saying, "I am willing. Be clean." Immediately, the man was cleansed of his leprosy" (Matt. 8:3, NIV).

King David appealed to the desire of God for this kind of cleansing. When the leprosy of sin had disfigured him, he prayed, "You desire truth in the inward being; therefore teach me wisdom in my secret heart.... Create in me a clean heart, O God, and put a new and right spirit within me..." (Ps. 51:6a, 10). Anytime we come to God with a deep longing for inner cleansing from sin, we appeal to the greatest desire of God's heart. God responds lovingly and fully because this is his will for us.

Holiness is seen in the call of God

It was old, rugged Peter who, after many years of proving the promises of God, wrote, "But just as he who called you is holy, so be holy in all you do, for it is written, 'Be holy for I am holy'" (1 Pet. 1:15-16). With a fisherman's firm grip, Peter had grabbed both the Old Testament (Lev. 11:44, 45; 19:2; 20:7) and what soon would be the New Testament and pulled them together in one strong and continuous cord of holiness. He knew that, as Samuel Brengle once noted, "God is in earnest about this. It is God's [call] and it cannot be evaded."[5]

We are persuaded that, if a clarion call to holiness were put out again by those who know God, we would see less separation between faith and life, less discoloring of God's will for us, fewer statements like the one from the young man planning to sin every weekend. Such planning dishonors the holy God who seeks to penetrate our lives with the pure color of holy love.

Holiness is seen in the people of God

Both the Old and New Testaments are filled with the testimonies of men and women who, despite their shortcomings, were transformed by the holiness of God. These heroes of the faith did not always perform perfectly, nor are they painted as some kind of super beings blessed with supernatural powers far beyond the normal. Even the clay feet of the revered King David are graphically reported, dirt and all. What set them apart was the orientation of their hearts—they "walked with God," "found favor in the eyes of the LORD," "did all that the LORD had commanded him," "did right in the sight of the Lord," "had a different spirit and followed me fully," and "was blameless, upright, fearing God, and turning away from evil." By faith Enoch "walked with God; then he was no more, because God took him" (Gen. 5:23-24). Then, "By faith Enoch was taken so that he did not experience death; and he was not found, because God had taken him. For it was attested before he was taken away that 'he had pleased God'" (Gen. 5:23-24; Heb. 11:5).

Faith is not walking around on one leg. James encouraged two-legged Christians when he spoke of faith *and* works—one without the other is dead (James 2:17). Peter understood the holy, the whole faith walk, saying, "but like the Holy One who called you, be holy yourselves also in all your behavior; because it is written, 'You shall be holy, for I am holy'" (1 Pet. 1:15-16, NASB).

Salvation cannot be achieved by works, nor can holiness, but holiness always issues in good works. It is possible for a human being to so walk with God in this life that God can take him/her directly to heaven without having to cleanse him/her through death or purgatory. The beauty of holiness in Enoch's life was so clear and pure that God simply transferred him into his Kingdom--because the Kingdom of God was already in him. Christians with spiritual integrity evidence holiness in their daily living.

Holiness is seen in the breath of God

Holiness is not something we put on like a coat, wearing God around the hallways and streets of our lives. Holiness is the fullness of God in us. It is what got "in us" that got us into trouble in the beginning. This sin orientation must now be replaced by a Spirit relationship that displaces and refills.

When we sinned against God, the very breath of God was lost to us. Since that time it has been God's aim to restore in us the very breathing of God's Spirit. David's greatest concern in his penitent prayer recorded in Psalm 51:10-12 was that he might lose God's presence. In desperation he cries, "Create in me a clean heart, O God, and put a new and right spirit within me. Do not cast me away from your presence, and do not take your holy spirit from me. Restore to me the joy of your salvation, and sustain in me a willing spirit." The Spirit of God is the breath, the source, the dynamic, the joy of God's holy salvation that is to be present and pulsating within us.

We humans were made to breathe easily. Not being able to get the next breath is a horrible feeling. Breathing is one of the most natural and important functions of the physical body. Without air, we soon die. The light grows dim and finally goes out. All color drains away as the breath departs. An elderly lady who had grown up on a farm shared the agony of watching her hard-working father struggle for air because of bronchial asthma. Literally suffocating to death, the image of his suffering fixed itself in her young mind, and especially the horror of his last, gasping words, saying, "More air!"

We cannot live without breath. When we need it, there is nothing tastier, more delightful, and more satisfying than a deep breath. The same is true with the soul. Without the breath of God, we suffocate. King David, struggling to get his next breath, cried out to the Lord, "More air!—Let me breathe again! Don't take your Holy Spirit [your divine breath] from me." The church ought to be deeply concerned about this. Many are dying for lack of divine breath, and some of them are doing so right in the church. We suffer a dimming of the spiritual eyes because we have lost the breath of life—the person, presence, and power of the Holy Spirit. Our prayer must be—"More air!"

Dennis Kinlaw points out that the Holy Spirit is called "Holy" because of what He does in us.[6] Ezekiel prophesied about the divine intent for the seed of Abraham (which includes the church): "I will sanctify my great name, which has been profaned among the nations, and which you have profaned among them; and the nations shall know that I am the Lord, says the Lord God, when through you I display my holiness before their eyes.... A new heart I will give you, and a new spirit I will put within you; and I will remove from your body the heart of stone and give you a heart of flesh" (Ezek. 36:23-27).

It is with this same intent that Jesus faced the agony of the cross, anticipated the hope of the resurrection, and spoke of the eternal purpose of God. It all led to baptism with the Holy Spirit. Jesus told his disciples "to wait there for the promise of the Father. 'This,' he said, 'is what you have heard from me; for John baptized with water, but you will be baptized with the Holy Spirit not many days from now'" (Acts 1:4-5). Jesus focused on the vital importance of the person and presence of the Holy Spirit in the lives of all future disciples (Jn. 14-16). He even said, "I tell you the truth: it is to your advantage that I go away, for if I do not go away, the Advocate [Comforter, Spirit] will not come to you; but if I go, I will send him to you" (Jn. 16:7).

This sending of the enlivening Spirit is behind Ezekiel 37, that dramatic vision of dry bones. The question rested on the very power of God to bring life—"can these bones live again?" (Ezek. 37:3). Then the Spirit of the Lord told the prophet to speak to the bones, telling them to "hear the word of the Lord. Thus says the Lord God to these bones: I will cause breath to enter you, and you shall live" (Ezek. 37:4-5). And so they did, and so can we!

The Holy Spirit is God's breath within the soul. This is the very life of God in us, wanting to burst forth in the bountiful and beautiful fruit of God's Spirit. If the Spirit of God is God in our lives, we will bear the fruit of the Spirit because this is who God is and this is the colorful feast of God's presence. God is indwelling love, joy, peace, patience, kindness, goodness, faithfulness, gentleness, and self-control (Gal. 5:22-23). The Apostle Paul declares, "If we live by the Spirit, let us also walk by the Spirit" (Gal. 5:25). As Peter puts it, "His divine power has granted to us everything pertaining to life and godliness" (2 Pet. 1:3). Our proper holiness prayer? Oh God, let us breath again! Let us be filled with the blessed fruit of your Spirit's cleansing, gifting, and guiding presence.

Holiness is seen in the wisdom of God

James writes, "If any of you is lacking in wisdom, ask God, who gives to all generously and ungrudgingly, and it will be given you" (1:5). The wisdom in question is not the kind that the world looks for, as in "worldly-wise" which James says is filled with "envy and selfish...disorder" (3:16). Such wayward wisdom sounds like the accusation Paul makes of the church at Corinth: "You are still worldly. For since there is jealousy and quarreling among you, are you not worldly?" (1 Cor. 3:3, NIV). Such supposed wisdom, James says, "does not come down from above, but is earthly, unspiritual, devilish" (3:15).

The wisdom James urges us to ask for is a wisdom far higher—its source is none other than God: "But the wisdom that comes from heaven is first of all pure; then peace-loving, considerate, submissive, full of mercy and good fruit, impartial and sincere" (3:17, NIV). What a colorful list! These are holy colors of God. James says that this "wisdom that comes from heaven is first of all pure." This pure color of holiness is what fills every other color with its brilliant purity.

Wisdom according to the Bible is directly related to understanding. It is seeing the unseen spiritual reality, a holy God, and responding accordingly. Job notes that God once said to the human race, "Truly, the fear of the Lord, that is wisdom; and to depart from evil is understanding" (28:28). Wisdom is the moral compass that keeps us pointed in the right direction.

This is what Proverbs considers the bottom line: "Trust in the Lord with all your heart, and do not rely on your own insight. In all your ways acknowledge him, and he will make straight your paths. Do not be wise in your own eyes; fear the Lord, and turn away from evil.... The fear of the Lord is the beginning of wisdom, and the knowledge of the Holy One is insight" (3:5-7; 9:10). It is impossible to keep our moral practices sound and our inward attitudes right while our heart clashes with the holy ways of God.

A missionary couple serving in Buenos Aires, Argentina, had a calling to reach the upper class for Christ. They prayed for guidance. The wife happened to be involved with a company that had a promotional approach called "Color Me Beautiful." It matched dress colors to a person's skin tones. She quickly found this an open door to fashion-conscious people. Soon she was leading many of these people into the knowledge of the One who could color them beautiful on the inside.

The Apostle Paul said that "the mind that is set on the flesh is hostile to God; it does not submit to God's law—indeed it cannot, and those who are in the flesh cannot please God" (Rom. 8:7-8). His answer to this clash is simple—to set our minds on the Spirit rather than the flesh (Rom. 8:5). Through the Spirit, God will "color me beautiful" with "the wisdom that comes from heaven," a color that "is first of all pure; then peace-loving, considerate, submissive, full of mercy and good fruit, impartial and sincere" (Jam. 3:17, NIV).

What an offer from God. All we have to do is ask, "If any of you is lacking in wisdom, ask God, who gives to all generously and ungrudgingly, and it will be given you" (Jam. 1:5). The color of holiness is seen in receiving the wisdom of God. Color me holy!

Holiness is seen in the prayers to God

The Bible is a prayer book that unlocks the ways to inner cleansing. Many Christian songs have been inspired by biblical prayer themes, especially those for cleansing, wholeness, purity, and divine likeness—for holiness! Here are select words from a few:

> Give me a heart like yours...
>
> Cleanse me from every sin, and set me free...
>
> Holy Spirit, breathe on me, until my heart is clean...
>
> Breathe on me, breath of God, until my heart is pure...
>
> My deepest prayer, my highest goal, that I may be like Jesus...
>
> Oh, to be like you, this is my constant longing and prayer...
>
> Lord, I loathe myself and sin; enter now and make me clean...
>
> Let the beauty of Jesus be seen in me...
>
> Lord reign in me—over every thought, over every word.
>
> Purify my heart—Take me to the cross.
>
> Change my heart, make it ever true.
>
> May my life reflect the beauty of the Lord.

Sadly, in so many of our lives, these song prayers, although beautiful and powerful, end up like so many prayed without much thought. We say them but really have no expectation of their actually being answered. These prayers can be lovely words without immediate meaning. Some offer them as a standard preparation for worship, but with no expectation of real life about to be received. They make people feel better without being better.

Here are critical song lyrics: "O thou Spirit divine, all my nature refine 'till the beauty of Jesus be seen in me." This prayer is not necessarily something always believed, just routinely mouthed. It satisfies the conscience without sanctifying the soul. This is the highway to religion without holiness, religion without a transforming divine-human relationship. It is holiness hoped for without being sought after earnestly until actually received.

What if God were allowed to actually answer such sanctification prayers? Imagine what that would do to the church if answers were frequent? It would bring a tsunami, a tidal wave, not of destruction but of transformation. Can you imagine what it would do to families and our society? David believed that if his prayer were answered it would deeply affect those around him. He prayed, "Then I will teach transgressors your ways, and sinners will return to you" (Ps. 51:13). The heart of David's prayer is in verses 6-13:

> You desire truth in the inward being;
>
> therefore teach me wisdom in my secret heart.
>
> Purge me with hyssop, and I shall be clean;
>
> wash me, and I shall be whiter than snow....
>
> Create in me a clean heart, O God,
>
> and put a new and right spirit within me....
>
> Then I will teach transgressors your ways,
>
> and sinners will return to you.

The cry is to be made into a beauty even whiter than snow, true holiness restored.

David's prayer is akin to Peter's brokenness after his denials of Jesus—he went out and wept bitterly. It is the kind of prayer that gets to the core of the problem with the same honesty, humility, and fervency that Saul (Paul) gained from his experience on the road to Damascus. God had told Simeon to go to him "because he is praying." The idea is, "Look at this! This man is really praying!" Saul was a Pharisee of the Pharisees, as he put it, and one thing Pharisees did was pray. He had prayed countless prayers in his life, but all of a sudden he is *really praying*.

When I (Hubert) was a young pastor in northern Indiana, I was visited by my conference superintendent. Some days later he was driving me somewhere and commented about his visit to hear me preach. I waited for some words of praise and affirmation, but what he said stunned me. "Hubert, I heard you preach, and you don't have any unction (anointing), do you?" I was so taken back that I didn't know what to say. On my return home, I told my wife what he had said, expecting some support, but I got none. I walked over to the church, stood at the front and prayed, "Lord, is what he said true?"

The answer was immediate—"Yes." So I fell on my knees at the front pew and began to pray like I had never prayed in my life. I heard God say, "Look at this! He's *really praying*." I asked God to "create in me a clean heart." I asked for God's Holy Spirit." The Spirit came and said, "Be clean!" God came to my heart that day in a definite way, establishing a process of spiritual development that would cause me to surrender to the molding of God, making me more and more like Jesus.

We have learned that "the Lord disciplines those whom he loves, and chastises every child whom he accepts" (Heb. 12:6). As someone said, God disciplines us to increase our fruit and chastises us to decrease our faults. There has been a surrender at life's core. Many of the great joys of our lives in the church will flow only from such surrender.

One of the wildest things we know is watching a rodeo, especially the bull-riding contest. The attempts of the animal to throw off the rider are incredible. How different this is from the steer-lassoing contest where the horse follows the will of its rider. The disciplined horse thinks only of working for its master. The difference is in submission. The horse could be fully trained because it had submitted its will to the owner's will—something so unlike those bulls!

One of the great problems we face in discipling believers is dealing with Christians who still have the kick in them (the bucking bronco of the rodeo with no surrender). They learn with difficulty and seem to go back over the same failure again and again. An amazing thing happens to learning and growth once full surrender to the will and ways of God has taken place. It is what David was speaking of when he prayed, "Restore to me the joy of your salvation, and sustain in me a willing spirit. Then I will teach transgressors your ways, and sinners will return to you" (Ps. 51:12-13). Holiness is a willing spirit.

There was urgency in the prayer of Jesus for his disciples: "I am not asking you [the Father] to take them out of the world, but I ask you to protect them from the evil one. They do not belong to the world, just as I do not belong to the world. Sanctify them in the truth; your word is truth" (Jn. 17:15-17). It is with this same urgency that the Apostle Paul prays for the church: "May the God of peace himself sanctify you entirely; and may your spirit and soul and body be kept sound and blameless at the coming of our Lord Jesus Christ. The one who calls you is faithful, and he will do this" (1 Thess. 5:23-24).

If King David prayed this way for himself, and Jesus prayed this way for his disciples, and the Apostle Paul prayed this way for the church, we ought to give ourselves to such prayers. They will bring an answer because they rise out of God's heart for us. Will you unleash the answer to God's prayer for your heart? Would you pray and believe that God will "color me beautiful"? It begins with the Bible prayer used in a beautiful Christian hymn:

> Search me, O God, and know my heart today.
>
> Try me, O Savior; know my thoughts I pray.

See if there be some wicked way in me;

Cleanse me from every sin, and set me free.

Lord, take my life, and make it wholly Thine;

Fill my poor heart with Thy great love divine.

Take all my will, my passion, self, and pride.

I now surrender; Lord, in me abide.[7]

Amen! So be it Lord!

Notes

[1] The 2012 book *Heart and Life* (eds. Barry Callen and Don Thorsen, Aldersgate Press) probes with skill the several dimensions of Christian holiness that are critical to the life of today's churches.

[2] See this elaborated in Barry L. Callen, *Caught Between Truths: The Central Paradoxes of Christian Faith* (Emeth Press, 2007).

[3] See this truth elaborated in Barry L. Callen, *Beneath the Surface: Reclaiming the Old Testament for Today's Christians* (Emeth Press, 2012). Note especially the "holiness stream" of biblical teaching.

[4] Hymn "Let the Beauty of Jesus be Seen in Me," author unknown (no copyright).

[5] Commissioner Samuel Logan Brengle was an evangelist in the Salvation Army in the early 1900s and widely known for his speaking and writing ability. Five of his insightful books are *Helps to Holiness, Heart Talks on Holiness, The Way of Holiness, The Soul-Winner's Secret, and When the Holy Ghost is Come.*

[6] This was heard often in his preaching, lectures and writing. Dr. Dennis Kinlaw served as president of Asbury College and the Francis Asbury Society. He has authored *The Mind of Christ* and *We Live as Christ*, among several other outstanding books that give a clarion call to the Christian holiness message.

[7] Verses one and three of the hymn "Cleanse Me" by J. Edwin Orr.

Holiness.... Off Course

Church History

Chapter 4

Dark Distortions

I am not afraid that people called Methodists would ever cease to exist in Eu-rope or America. But I am afraid lest they should only exist as a dead sect, having the form of religion without the power.   —John Wesley

It is as sad as it is true. Somehow the lovely shades of God's holy beauty have gotten spoiled. While clearly biblical, holy living has not always been seen in everyday church life. Like John Wesley feared (see above), there can be holiness in name only, a "dead sect" that still has the form but not the power, the words without the reality. God's people have been distracted, darkened, drained of the bright divine colors. There remains an evil that pulls the wrong way. Evil is "live" spelled backwards; the Evil One is ever active to turn things around, upside down, bringing the counterfeit to replace the true.

Even the best things can go wrong. They can sour, lose their joyous color, fade into dissension and disuse. This happened among Christians who comprised later generations of the people who first were inspired by the nineteenth-century Holiness Movement in North America and England. One important way of helping to bring about a new day in today's church is to understand what went wrong in the distant and more recent past. Holiness? Of course! But holiness, so central to biblical teaching and the very heart of God, has also gone off course.

A Darkness Descended

What happened? Society certainly changed. Change appears inevitable and can bring confusion among serious Christians. What is permanent and what is passing in how faith is to be applied to life and a given society's norms and needs?

In recent decades we have watched a rapidly shifting culture in North America. The population has become much more pluralistic. Record immigration has brought unparalleled racial and ethnic diversity. Hispanics overtook African Americans as the largest minority in the United States. "Gay" rights and same-sex marriage have gained considerable ground with the general public. Women have achieved a higher status in the workplace. The traditional family unit has been compromised by frequent divorces and the unconventional—gay couples, stepparents, single parents, and awkwardly blended families. Electronic cash, entertainment on demand, and legalized gambling have become the social norm, and also have become accompanied by heavy debt loads, high anxiety, and sedative pills to help the masses cope. The dominance of Christianity in the culture has melted away.

So much in public life has become bigger, louder, and more outrageous. In the middle of it all, there also has emerged a personal emptiness that longs for filling and an individualism that longs for real community. While life has been moving at a faster pace, people are living longer and trying hard to look younger. Cell phones now allow constant communication from anywhere to anywhere, and our GPS units (global positioning systems) have begun keeping track of where we were and are going—immediately, but not long-term. In fact, we now are always found, but more frequently feel lost. We are more obese in the midst of an exercising and dieting boom. We are increasingly tolerant, and yet still so tribalized that war continues to devastate the earth. So much is new; sadly, however, most basic things are still the same.

Church people have been stressed in the midst of all this change. They have become confused about what the Bible means by "holiness"—or they have decided it is impossible to receive and live. Is it even necessary for people living in very different times? The holiness passion of yesterday has become today's embarrassment, or at least it has fallen into a confusion not well understood. So, in numerous places, the subject is being left largely unaddressed.

Even more has been pulling against the holiness preaching that was commonly heard in the great holiness revivals of the nineteenth century. Sin back then had been made to sound like a ugly substance stuck in the soul that could be "eradicated" entirely and instantly by an act of radical commitment and cleansing. Definitional, psychological, and timing questions now have been raised about the adequacy of the assumptions that lay behind such claims and language. Further, too many believers made great claims about their spiritual attainments and then led lives that argued against the claims. The public was quick to judge that fancy words not obvious in faithful living are worse than saying nothing.

John Wesley, great advocate of Christian holiness, spoke sharply against relying for religious credibility on religious words and traditional churchly actions. In fact, in his sermon "The Nature of Enthusiasm" he suggests that a person existing only on the surface of the faith is hardly a Christians at all. Why? "For Christians are holy, these are unholy; Christians love God, these love the world. Christians are humble, these are proud; Christians are gentle, these are passionate; Christians have the mind which was in Christ, these are at the utmost distance from it. Consequently, they are no more Christians than they are archangels."

Christian believers may claim the merits of church involvement and proper Christian opinions as grounds for their Christian beliefs and identity. However, as Wesley made clear in that sermon on "Enthusiasm," Christian identity is not as it should be until there is clear evidence of a person having "tasted the love of God." Based on Galatians 6:3, he warned believers not to think too highly of themselves, whatever their accomplishments or associations. Indeed, he called on all believers to press on toward "perfection," the high calling of experiencing the life-changing presence of God.

Spoiled Colors

Times have changed and so did the commitments of many Christian people. The Holiness Movement of the nineteenth century, wonderful as it was in many ways, slowly institutionalized and either radicalized in isolation from "the world" or compromised with the world. There were negative developments on the theological front that brought a dullness to the bright luster of earlier generations of holiness people. As the twentieth century wore on, the very optimistic expectations of "entire sanctification" became less and less credible in the light of the apparently intractable nature of sin. By the 1950s "the extravagant promises of the grace of entire sanctification began to be tempered."[1] Theologians attempted to redefine the "sin" that supposedly could be "eradicated," narrowing its definition and expanding the list of "infirmities" that are an inescapable consequence of fallen humanity.

It is important to realize that concepts and words used for theological issues can become dated and misleading. "Holiness" is an uncommon word today, one that tends to trigger unpleasant images of hypocritical people claiming more religious status and than has actually taken root in their lives. They have what sound like arrogant and empty testimonies that relate only to some other world. When they speak their elevated language, people in their presence are made to feel put down. No wonder sensitive holiness advocates wishing to draw believers to the grand holiness ideal began shying away from the traditional language of their treasured holiness tradition.

Language about holiness certainly has become a problem. Classic phrases like "Christian perfection," "entire sanctification," and "the second blessing" are rarely used today by either preacher or layperson. Jesus did not use this exact language. It was common a few generations back but rarely is heard even in today's "holiness" churches—and despite earlier belief that such language seeks to describe a distinctive doctrine that is soundly biblical in origin. Now there is fear that, at least in North America, denominations with histories in the holiness tradition have become virtually unrecognizable from the "Evangelical" mainstream of doctrinal teaching and Christian living. Language is of secondary importance, of course; locating and somehow naming the spiritual reality is what is crucial.

More than this has been going on at the level of the average person in the pew. People—especially younger people—have grown tired of the negative results of holiness teaching and practice that seemed to them to have gone off course, gotten off-color by extreme emphases and erratic follow through. Many within the Baby Boomer generations have reacted against inconsistencies and "weird" expectations. They have rejected personal "convictions" that rigid people hold as a standard of right and wrong for everyone. Too much emotional hype about holiness has led to too much hypocrisy or, again, so it often has seemed. There has come to be less patience with claims of instant spiritual perfection, attitudes of religious arrogance, and lists of life prohibitions tied mostly to given cultural settings, or even to personal preferences put into the mouth of God.

I (Barry) fell in love and married a young woman from a very conservative holiness congregation. No woman in my home church was allowed to sing in the choir if there were any visible make-up on her face—thought to be an inappropriate painting of pride on cheeks and lips. I was a young ministerial student with some leadership experience, but soon I was informed that I was not welcome to step foot on the chancel area of my new wife's home church. Why? Had I done something morally wrong? No. I was being faced with a spiritual principle gone wrong, an application of holiness that was resisting the very practice of holiness.

The problem was that I was now wearing a wedding ring, a simple band that cost less than twenty dollars. It was being claimed that the sight of that ring was evidence of more than my being married. It showed my readiness to waste my substance on "gold, pearls, and costly array." I earlier had been banned by my parents from visiting the local bowling alley, a "worldly" diversion. What was said to be wrong with rolling heavy balls down a lane of polished wood? Nothing, except that the local "sinners" hung out there and being with them would give "the appearance of evil." Christians, so it was being said, should be holy in part by associating only with the known holy—even though Jesus did otherwise and paid a heavy price for showing great concern for people like prostitutes and tax collectors.

Perversions of holiness precept and practice grew numerous over time. Sometimes quite subtly, they have sucked the blood out of the body, leaving a corpse without the color of the holy life of the divine. Some of the sad results are noted in the 2006 "Holiness Manifesto." This pivotal document was produced by the Wesleyan Holiness Consortium, a large gathering of Christians from many denominations who are convinced that a revival of holiness teaching and practice is the necessary dynamic for renewal in today's churches.

This pivotal manifesto understandably decries "our petty lines of demarcation," the tendency to "institutionalism," the pain of "infighting among followers of Jesus." What is needed now, it counters, is a resurgence of *biblical* holiness, the kind full of the "unifying power of God that transforms," the kind that should be present in all Christians in all times and places. Holiness, when biblically defined and Christ-like in nature, will unite and not divide. We write this book in hope of pointing again to the bright, clear, promise-laden rainbow of God's holiness. We hope to encourage new commitment to holy living after the storms that have caused many to scatter and fall away.

There is some good news on today's religious scene. Despite the problems, compromises, confusions, and frustrations experienced by many holiness people of past generations (or at least with which they have been associated), Christians today are making something known more and more. They are ready for something better than they have, something authentic, life-changing, and church-expanding. They long for faith experiences and congregations with a real spiritual difference. They want to be and do what will benefit and attract the world around them for Christ. They are tired of driving people away by throwing at non-church people critical, judgmental, "holier-than-thou" attitudes. Such attitudes are far from "the mind of Christ." Are they done with holiness? No, they are ready for true holiness. They want to see the beautiful rainbow of God received and lived out.

Whatever "holiness" language is or is not used, whatever religious institutions are joined or abandoned, honest and hurting people want to actually be new people "in Christ," people who then can impact the world for good. Frustrated church people want to be linked with fellow believers who really care, deeply love, and are prepared to serve unselfishly. They want to be believers who are clearly different because they walk with a holy God who is coloring them with healing grace and sending them out as credible carriers of truly good news.

Perhaps, as one church leader recently observed, Western culture "is nearing a point where the Christian faith can be successfully reintroduced. Maybe the collapse of the present order will lead to a new outbreak of revolutionary [holiness-oriented] Christianity."[2] Holiness? Of course! It is thoroughly biblical even if it has been practiced poorly at times, injuring the beauty of the intended witness of the Spirit. We cannot, because of a poor showing, dismiss this important subject and its substantial possibilities for healthy spiritual life, growing churches, and social relevance.

Holiness is about serious believers in Jesus Christ who are forming communities of faith that reflect the Spirit of Christ and are actively about the Spirit's agenda in the world. God wants a people "who will dare to be his own, trust him, love him, and risk for him, in short, who will be like God in character and with God as God works redemptively in this world."[3] To be such a people will require brutal honesty and humility about our view of the Word of God, our theological predispositions, and our personal preferences.

> Holiness is about serious believers in Jesus Christ who are forming communities of faith that reflect the Spirit of Christ and are actively about the Spirit's agenda in the world.

A good way to recognize such honesty and humility is to recall what John Wesley called the "marks" or "character" of a Methodist. He was not being "denominational." What he wanted for Methodists is what should mark every Christian of any affiliation. He emphasized being "real Christians,"[4] sincere believers whose identity and integrity are not found in particular opinions or names or laying stress on any part of the Gospel to the exclusion of others. There should be biblical balance and there will be cultural and personality diversity among believers, differences sometimes not appreciated in religious life because they are classed as "sin" when not agreed to by local leaders who resist any differences.

Tension of True and False

Differences there always will be, but some things should always be the same and be seen in all Christians. John Wesley believed that authentic Christianity has some distinguishing characteristics that set Christians apart. If they are not present, whatever a believer's testimony may claim, holiness is not present or at least has gone off-color. Spiritual life without these characteristics is not mature, healthy, fragrant and beautiful. He was sure that a truly holy life will be very noticeable and desirable. The obvious results in our lives are the intended "marks," the fruit of faithfulness. If the marks look other than they should, holiness has been compromised and its witness weakened.

The following are characteristics or marks to be sought when proceeding down the Christian path of authentic holiness. They are guidelines for resisting the dark distortions.

We are to live by the power of Christ

Negative stereotypes have gathered around holiness and pentecostal people (many of whom are also holiness people). Follow the "method" and get the assured result, instant sanctification or a desired spiritual gift. Do mouth and voice training and you will get the tongues gift. If you will just come, it will be done. But holiness is not primarily the result of our efforts, our discipline and faithfulness, a set formula, our desired spiritual gifts. Whatever spiritual heights are gained, pride and arrogance over "our" achievements are always inappropriate. Humility is the constant mark of holiness. We know that "every good gift cometh from above" (Jam. 1:17).

The Apostle Paul tied heart renewal directly to the resurrection of Jesus. His heart passion was, "I want to know Christ and the power of his resurrection" (Ph. 3:10). A resurrection is something no human being can make happen. It rests solely on the power of God. When Lazarus was raised from the dead, people came from all around to see him—not because of what he had done but because of what Jesus had done. There was nothing for this man to glory in except that he lived again by the power of Christ. This was Christ's gift to him and he was a living testimony of "abundant life."

Any supposed holiness tainted with self-importance is simply not holiness of the Christian sort. James Bishop, a pioneer missionary to India with World Gospel Mission, opened the South India Bible Institute in 1937 with the motto "SAVED TO SERVE." The students were too poor to hire servants, so they did all the cleaning, marketing, and "sweeper" work themselves. Sweeping was for the "untouchables" (cleaning latrines and sewers and handling refuse). A high-caste student, recently converted to Christ, consistently skipped his turn sweeping. Without a word of reproof, Rev. Bishop, although the house father, lone teacher, and school principal, did the repulsive work in his stead. Personified humility and love broke the boy's heart. The Savior who washed the feet of his disciples came even closer to this new convert as he now willingly bent to do the work of an outcaste.

God is no respecter of persons. The most humble and truly holy people are those who have been touched by the glorious color of God's loving character. They do not exalt themselves with a public show of their gifts, knowing well their divine source and serving intent. They do not segregate themselves with their class, race, tribe, education, or means, but mingle gladly with "the least of these." More than anyone else, they know that all is from God, and so they walk humbly before the Lord their God, showing the true beauty of holiness.

> The most humble and truly holy people are those who have been touched by the glorious color of God's loving character.

Our commitment to Christ must be complete

Holiness people often have lived on the margins of mainstream society, and thus have been looked down upon by the establishment—secular and religious. While poverty and powerlessness are hardly to be desired, the reverse certainly can be a threat to true holiness. Note the Wesley quote that leads this chapter. He also once warned: "As wealth has increased in the history of the church, the mind of Christ has diminished in the same measure."[5]

If holiness is anything, it is being "all-in" for Christ. One who is complete in Christ should not be double-minded, not be flitting like a bird going back and forth from one branch to another. The clear call is, "Choose this day whom you will serve" (Josh. 24:15). Jesus insisted that no person can serve two masters (Lk. 16:13). One who is holy has the love of God shed abroad in the heart by the Holy Spirit. The holy one loves the Lord with all the heart. A mature believer cannot be double-minded.

Holiness is a call of one-hundred percent. Joshua affirmed this truth to his people by saying, "Take good care to observe the commandment and instruction that Moses the servant of the Lord commanded you, to love the Lord your God, to walk in all his ways, to keep his commandments, and to hold fast to him, and to serve him with all your heart and with all your soul" (22:5). He insisted that God's people must "hold fast to the Lord your God... Be very careful...to love the Lord your God" (22:8, 11), being sure never to "turn aside...to the right hand or to the left" (22:6).

It is difficult to say how much of premarital counseling sticks with young couples. Most have their thoughts on their dreams more than on what the counselor is saying. But, if nothing else, there is one thing any counselor should help young couples see. Marriage is about one-hundred percent, especially in three vital areas—love, faithfulness and purity. Just because some have lowered the standard does not change the truth. Dare any of us say to a fiancé, "I want you to know that I love you 90%." Such will not work. The same is true in our commitment to Christ. It is all or nothing!

I (Hubert) saw my mother, a first-term missionary in Bolivia, make a very hard decision. My parents were asked to move to a remote jungle station. With my father away in meetings, my mother undertook this move alone with four children and a guide. It was a horrific trip and the little house where we were to live was not finished and filled with mosquitoes. Later, the family possessions arrived, worse for the wear having been pulled through swamps by oxcart. Mother decided that she could not remain in this God-forsaken place—this is, until she saw in one of the boxes a plaque that said, "Only one life, 'twill soon be past; only what's done for Christ will last." She knelt and renewed her commitment that "even if I die here, I will love and serve you." Had God in Christ not given all for us? To be holy is to give all in return.

Our attitudes and actions must conform to Christ

Holy people sometimes isolate themselves from the unholy, thinking that separation protects the holiness from contamination. But John Wesley insisted on the more biblical perspective—there is no holiness that is not *social* holiness. E. Stanley Jones agreed: "An individual gospel without a social gospel is a soul without a body. A social gospel without an individual gospel is a body without a soul. One is a ghost, the other is a corpse."[6] Walking close to Jesus should (must) shape one's thoughts and actions and relationships. Complete commitment brings significant conformity to the mind of Christ.

Forgiveness is something we receive by grace. Holiness is something we live by God's grace *and* our commitment. God's intent for each believer is not only to remove the guilt of sins committed, but to change our very nature, granting the power to live victorious Christian lives, loving God with all our hearts and our neighbors as ourselves. Here is where a Christian's life is lived in high-definition color. Too often Christians have settled into the culture of "the forgiven" (forgiveness is all that matters) rather than going on to the full-rainbow call to holiness in its private and necessarily social dimensions.

Spiritual life is stunted when one does not come out of the prayer closet or down from the mountain with the transfigured Jesus and go down into the valley where the mass of humanity struggles with life and faith, hunger and thirst. The beauty and hope of Christ must be taken to where the people are. Staying clear of the pain and confusion is the world's way. The Christian mandate is: "Do not be conformed to this world, but be transformed by the renewing of your minds, so that you may discern what is the will of God—what is good and acceptable and perfect" (Rom. 12:2). According to God who sent Jesus to us, the holy way is to love the world sacrificially whatever the personal consequences.

This is where so many crash and burn. It is much easier to lay claim to forgiveness than to holiness. Forgiveness is something we receive. Holiness is something we live, always with God and others in mind. They go hand in hand, and anyone who does not take hold of both hands does not know the fullness of God's grace—grace wanting to remove the guilt of sins committed and to change our very nature, granting us power to live victorious Christian lives, to love God with all our hearts and our neighbors as ourselves.

> Has God in Christ not given all for us? To be holy is to give all in return.

Jesus said this about "false prophets." "You will know them by their fruits. Are grapes gathered from thorns, or figs from thistles? In the same way, every good tree bears good fruit, but the bad tree bears bad fruit. A good tree cannot bear bad fruit, nor can a bad tree bear good fruit. Every tree that does not bear good fruit is cut down and thrown into the fire. Thus you will know them by their fruits" (Mt. 7:16-20). There is falseness in anyone who claims to "live by the Spirit" but does not "walk by the Spirit" (Gal. 5:25, NASB).

Poor actions, especially toward others, usually follow bad attitudes. If we have feelings of bitterness or hatred against someone, our actions toward them will usually go wrong. Paul admonished the church: "Have this attitude in yourselves which was also in Christ Jesus" (Phil. 2:5, NASB), and that attitude took him to a cross for our souls. "He humbled himself and became obedient to the point of death—even death on a cross" (Phil. 2:8). It is in this context that Paul says, "Do all things without murmuring and arguing, so that you may be blameless and innocent, children of God without blemish in the midst of a crooked and perverse generation, in which you shine like stars in the world" (Phil. 2:14-15).

Our need for a holy transformation into the likeness of Jesus Christ must not be diluted into something less demanding, less threatening, more manageable. There must be growth, accountability, integrity, authenticity, ethics, and service. All of these are critical and certainly help measure the presence and health of holiness. Only God creates in us new hearts and gives us a truly new way, the way of holiness.

Crossing the Color Divides

It is an irony that has plagued the world of Christian holiness. That which should unite has divided! The most deplorable thing within church life is the competing color differentiations. It is the *we-you* divide, denominationalism, racism, whatever *ism* forces apart what holiness should bring together.

True holiness is the road to repentance and reconciliation—not to harsh judgment of others and human division. In Christ's Spirit, there is to be unity beyond what the world can understand or duplicate: "For just as the body is one and has many members, and all the members of the body, though many, are one body, so it is with Christ. For in the one Spirit we were all baptized into one body—Jews or Greeks, slaves or free—and we were all made to drink of one Spirit" (1 Cor. 12:12-13).

More than we like to admit, whether our skins are black, yellow, red, brown or white, we have been prejudiced by our culture, made to carry the germs of false and divisive ideas from generation to generation. We bring harm to the cause of Christ when such things get into the church. Jesus himself became the target of various cultural and theological prejudices of his time, making him a stumbling block to belief in his person and mission (Rom. 9:32-33).

There are several stumbling stones that most of us have to deal with on our way to true Christianity. It is important that we identify them in order to deal with the issue before us—the tragedy of our "color divides." A classic illustration in the New Testament is the extra-ordinary life of Peter.

Jesus as the Messiah of the Jews

Jesus did not fit the traditional Jewish teaching. The more he contradicted that thinking the more many Jews stumbled and found belief impossible. When Peter confessed with the other disciples that Jesus was the Christ (Mk. 8:29), this was huge. The disciples had to overcome many obstacles to get to this point. But they still had only a limited idea of who Jesus really was. Soon their faith would be tested with some disturbing facts. This Christ was going to suffer and die (Mk. 8:31a). This became such an obstacle to their faith that they did not catch the promise that "after three days [the Son of Man] will rise again" (Mk. 8:31b). Jesus did not fit their idea of what a Messiah was supposed to do, so they forsook him.

Perhaps more than we realize or dare admit, Christians also come with "dark distortions" about this Jesus. Many who grew up in the church are not walking with Christ today because they encountered some Jesus-sized stumbling stones. Where do we go when our "Messiah" does not do what we want him to do? There are some very distorted ideas in the Christian world today of what we think the Messiah is supposed to do for us. Will we be made wealthy or whole, healthy in our bodies or holy in our souls? We are culturally conditioned and selfish, not yet colored with true holiness.

Jesus and a cross

Few Jewish people would have related the Messiah with death, and especially death on a cross. He was to be a conquering hero. But Jesus connected these ideas quite openly (Mk. 8:32a). Peter's scolding reaction was: "[He] took him [Jesus] aside and began to rebuke him" (Mk. 8:32). When Jesus would not back off of this cross thinking, the doubts began to find root in Peter's mind. His eventual denial of Jesus was totally honest when he said, "I do not know the man!" (Mt. 26:74).

It would be easy to cast stones at these disciples and their "dark distortions." But many of us do the same thing. How many have failed to see or accept the very basic purpose of God in Christ, resisting that same cross that Peter stumbled over? God's purpose? "Jesus also suffered outside the city gate in order to sanctify (literally, "make holy") the people by his own blood" (Heb. 13:12). How many sincere hearts, in their pursuit of this holiness, are rebuked by those Peters who think they are "in the know"?

Our human blindness

Peter was so prone to things of the flesh. You will remember that Jesus, on first meeting Peter who was called Simon, promised him that he would be called "Peter" (Jn. 1:42)—a piece of a rock—something strong, solid, and foundational, someone on whom the church would be built. Sadly, like any of us, Peter at first proved to be everything but that. It would take an amazing work of God to transform this man into someone useful to the kingdom of God, someone not wrapped up in self, someone reflecting God's own heart.

Years later, Peter, a man who now had embraced the sufferings of Christ in his own life, would write to a suffering church about this transformation. He introduced his second letter with powerful and revealing words that speak volumes: "Simon Peter, a bond-servant and apostle of Jesus Christ…" (2 Pet. 1:1). He was no longer a man given to the flesh but a man given to Christ. His journey of spiritual transformation had been long and difficult. He had to overcome an erratic personality and a blindness to the vision of Jesus for himself and the church. We must all walk this way—beyond ourselves to a vision of a holy life and church.

The problem of culture

From the day that new Jewish boys and girls came into the first-century world, they were indoctrinated with prejudices—as we all are. It was not only a part of their religious culture—to keep themselves undefiled—but it was part of their political culture. In keeping with the line of David, Jews despised being ruled by anyone but a Jew. There were "color" divides that were so much a part of their thinking. It was a culture of pride and isolation, a presumed holiness that fails to advance God's kingdom.

Jesus transcended this and was determined to change our cultural divides (the way we think and view the world). We are stuck in our ways of thinking, divided by tribe, language, politics, and religion. Each of these divisive forces has powerful effects on the way we look at and do things. But, with some hearts completely committed to him, Jesus began a process of exposing such cultural lies. We "liberated" twenty-first century moderns tend to think that we no longer have prejudices. We are ready to comfortably live and let live. But we are wrong.

I (Barry) once attended a very "liberal" seminary. It appeared to me that the only value that would not be tolerated by that faculty was the unwillingness of a student to tolerate nearly anything that some Christian wanted to believe or practice. I struggled with this cultural stance that was being labeled "enlightened" Christianity. Here is a difficult task—identifying and holding firmly to what is basic in the faith without being caught up in what is only a passing cultural preoccupation.

Peter struggled here. It took a vision from God (Acts 10) to convince him that Gentiles were not untouchables. And it would take a rebuke from the Apostle Paul to deal with the strong tendency to go back to his previous religious culture—especially when Peter's old friends were around. Paul made his point very public, saying, "But when Cephas [Peter] came to Antioch, I opposed him to his face, because he stood self-condemned; for until certain people came from James, he used to eat with the Gentiles. But after they came, he drew back and kept himself separate for fear of the circumcision faction. And the other Jews joined him in this hypocrisy, so that even Barnabas was led astray by their hypocrisy" (Gal. 2:11). Human prejudices die hard. We usually learn them early and carry them throughout our lives. Their darkness resists the bright light of holiness.

Laura taught primary children in the inner city of Chicago and was deeply loved by her third grade students. She was one of only a few Caucasian teachers in this mostly African-American school. One day, two of her students were arguing about whether she was white or black. One finally turned to Laura and said, "Miss Taube, you be black, right?" To which Laura responded, "No, I'm white." The child insisted strongly--"No, you be black!"

How sad that such racial prejudice had already been planted in that child's thinking; but how marvelous that this child was color blind when it came to love. No wonder God insists on love out of a pure heart. Paul knew this: "But the aim of [our] instruction is love that comes from a pure heart, a good conscience, and sincere faith" (1 Tim. 1:5). Love is the only antidote to the color divide, or any other kind of prejudicial divide. God aims to change our distorted cultural attitudes and behaviors with the reconciling grace that is holiness.

Will the real Jesus please stand up? Will you allow your best, your holy self to emerge through full commitment to the mind of Christ? Or will you instead slip back with Peter into old ways of separation and discrimination? Will you stand boldly with Paul and identify hypocrisy wherever it appears—including inside yourself? Will you walk the reconciling road of holiness, even if danger likely lurks somewhere down the way? Your courageous prayer should be— color me holy!

In the history of the United States, crossing one color divide has been difficult to say the least. It has been the presumed socially unacceptable mixing of black-skinned people with white-skinned people—in schools, marriages, restaurants, buses, wherever. This prejudice has gone so deep that it still taints somewhat the way we view each other. When the most segregated day of each week is Sunday, something is still wrong. How is it that those believers with white skin can feel so deeply about the desperate needs of "black Africa" and yet but hesitate to worship or fellowship with African Americans? Many of our prejudices still cross the oceans with missionaries and work teams carrying deep-seated thinking of subtle superiority. These prejudices must be faced and fought. It is only where the light of God's grace exposes our cultural lies that holiness can begin to shine, allowing for confession and change.

In recent years my (Barry) ministry has included the work of Horizon International on behalf of AIDS orphans. This has taken me to Africa where my white skin has put me in a minority racial category. A little orphan girl once sat on my lap in Zimbabwe fingering gently my bare arm. I was told that she was testing to see if the white would rub off! Miraculously, by God's grace alone, the white can be rubbed off—or should we say "washed off"—so that we are no longer known by the color of our skin but the love-color of our God, the rainbow brilliance of holiness. Paul said, "But the aim of [our] instruction is love that comes from a pure heart, a good conscience, and sincere faith" (1 Tim. 1:5). Here is the only antidote to prejudicial divides. God aims to change our distorted cultural behaviors by changing our hearts.

We must move into the Christian culture—in its purest sense—where in Christ there are no more Jew/Gentile, slave/free, or male/female divisions. This means erasing the artificial lines of discrimination, rendering all colors beautiful—"red, yellow, black and white, they are precious in God's sight." The Christian community should be a holy culture where all members truly celebrate their diversity and their unity in Christ. This then is a new people, a holy nation, the kingdom-of-God people.

> The Christian community should be a holy culture where all members truly celebrate their diversity and their unity in Christ.

The formative vision of the Church of God movement, my (Barry's) home church body, is seen in the web address of the new Wesleyan Holiness Consortium, *HolinessAndUnity.org*. Transformed lives, holy lives, should enable a unity among Christian believers that can transcend racial, tribal, and denominational lines and thereby enhance the church's mission in the world. As my (Barry's) dear friends James Earl Massey and Gilbert

W. Stafford sometimes said, "I belong to the whole church, and the whole church belongs to me."[7] John Wesley was transcending the artificial divisions established by us humans when he said, "The world is my parish." Similarly, the church is my home—all of it.

As we close this chapter on "Dark Distortions" we share classic words spoken of the One who can turn darkness into light. Mr. Beaver in C. S. Lewis' famous *The Chronicles of Narnia* says, "There's a right bit more than hope. Aslan...is on the move." "Safe?" said Mr. Beaver; "don't you hear what Mrs. Beaver tells you? Who said anything about safe? 'Course he [Aslan] isn't safe. But he's good. He's the King, I tell you. It's not as if he were a tame lion." These are words about the strong God who will shatter the dark distortions that have plagued our hearts since the fall of Adam and Eve. Holiness, pure and reconciling love, is the primary color of God. Color *me* holy, dear God!

Notes

[1] Mark Quanstrom, *A Century of Holiness Theology* (Beacon Hill Press of Kansas City, 2004), 11.

[2] Howard A. Snyder, *The Radical Wesley and Patterns of Church Renewal* (InterVarsity, 1980), preface.

[3] Barry L. Callen, "The Context: Past and Present," in *The Holiness Manifesto*, Kevin Mannoia and Don Thorsen, eds. (Eerdmans, 2008), 15.

[4] John Wesley sought in his own life to be a "real Christian." See his biography authored by Kenneth J. Collins and titled *A Real Christian: The Life of John Wesley* (Abingdon Press, 1999).

[5] *Works*, 13:260

[6] E. Stanley Jones, *A Song of Ascents: A spiritual Autobiography* (Abingdon Press, 1968, 151.

[7] See the chapter by John Smith and Gilbert Stafford, "Holiness and Unity: Fulfilling the Prayer of Jesus," in Barry Callen and Don Thorsen, eds., *Heart and Life: Rediscovering Holy Living* (Aldersgate Press, 2012).

Chapter 5

Blind Alleys

There's nobody living right, not even one, nobody who knows the score, no-body alert for God. They've all taken the wrong turn; they've all wandered down blind alleys. (Romans 3:10-12, *The Message*)

In the previous chapter we listed a range of ways that some Christian holiness advocates have gone off track. We remain sobered by Romans 3. There always is the warning that even those who have begun to walk the holiness path may make wrong turns, choose blind alleys, wind up not alert to God's intended way. Religion, even one with a holiness focus, can easily become an artificially set form that lacks the needed life-changing power.

The best of us has nothing to brag about. Henry Clay Morrison was president of Asbury College and then founder and president of Asbury Theological Seminary (1923-1942). A great champion of Christian holiness, he was appropriately humble about his own "accomplishments." He said this on his eighty-fourth birthday: "Looking backward, there is much to be thankful for, much to regret, and nothing to boast of. I think with gratitude of the countless mercies of God, his patience with an unworthy servant, and I go forward singing, 'Nothing in my hand I bring; simply to thy cross I cling'."[1] Here was a prominent holiness leader with a proper holiness attitude.

Recovering Pharisees

Every tradition of Christian spirituality, including the holiness one, is subject to spoilage. Often the ruin comes from zealots inside the tradition who push some aspect of its perspective to an extreme, thus distorting the whole. In the holiness tradition, the ruin sometimes comes from this faulty assumption--if God wants it, then it will just happen. In fact, God does indeed want our holiness, but *not without our help*.

I (Barry) remember with fondness a few occasions when I was a teenager spending the day with my father. Sometimes we would have fishing lines out each side of a boat, being pushed slowly along a lake's surface by a little motor (allowing the mosquitoes to stay up with us). At other times it was the two of us walking in formation through a snowy cornfield or brushy gully, following rabbit tracks and hoping to flush a furry animal into the open. By the time I was in college, these occasions with Dad became rare (and he died young). When they did come, I now only went hunting with him because I wanted exercise and the time with him. No longer did I carry a gun; I carried a camera and got different kinds of "shots" of living creatures. I needed food for the soul more than extra meat for the table. In a similar way, to be truly holy requires intentional time spent with the Father God. Nothing is automatic.

I (Hubert) remember well the testimony of a friend who had lived much of his Christian life roaming spiritual blind alleys. Holiness had become so distorted in his thinking and practice that it discolored his spirit and service. Then he had a "Peter" moment when God uncovered his distortions, showing him "a more perfect way." Feeling much like a recovering alcoholic, having to remove layer upon layer of law without liberty, he confessed to me concerning his journey, "I'm a recovering Pharisee."

"Pharisee" is what comes to mind as a description of those who make high claims to holiness of heart and life but are lacking the beauty (the Spirit/color) of holiness. We are unfair if we brand all Pharisees of Jesus' time as mere hypocrites. Many apparently were, but there also were those deeply sincere in their devotion to God. Like many Pharisees, the Apostle Paul, even before his conversion to Jesus, was radically committed to God and the Word of God. Although he had been a persecutor of the followers of Jesus, God granted him mercy because he did it ignorantly in unbelief (1 Tim. 1:13). He had a high, reverent regard for the Word of God and was, as he said, "as to righteousness under the law, blameless" (Phil. 3:6).

If we were to line up some of the qualities and characteristics of many Pharisees, they would land solidly in the "holiness" camp. We would welcome them into our fellowship because they had many values that we highly value. The Pharisees were strong advocates of right doctrine, gave liberally if not sacrificially, studied Scripture in a disciplined way, and preached purity of life. They certainly resisted the "humanism" of their day (Hellenism).

So why is it that we do not want to be associated with the Pharisees? Is it because Jesus butted heads with them? Probably, but why did Jesus have such a tough time with them? Why did the Pharisees have such a tough time with Jesus? Their deepest problem was a refusal to repent when their blind alleys were pointed out by Jesus. They were prisoners of pride. Many Pharisees stood their ground like blind men feeling around the wall of their own prison but not accepting the open door. Jesus called them "blind guides of the blind" (Matt. 15:14). Their holiness was off course. It is dangerous because it has the look of holiness without the heart of holiness. It holds to laws of holiness like air fresheners in a smoke-filled car, giving off a scent of something better but not really addressing the source of the problem.

A careful study of the Pharisees and Jesus' dealings with them reveals some of the blind alleys holiness people have gotten lost in. We need to understand these dark roads that lead nowhere.

Holding a standard that is *quantitative* rather than *qualitative*

Pharisees were keener on measuring spirituality by outward performance than by seeing or seeking inward purity. Appearances were paramount. The problem with this is that spiritual activity becomes a matter of ego rather than of the heart. God is no longer central and people are no longer primary, except to feed one's ego. Many ministries, whether church, missionary, or otherwise, have suffered at the hands of people seeking to impress rather than truly ministering for Jesus' sake. If it looks good on Facebook or in a resume, that is all that matters to some. To be able to share about overseas "ministry," to have a picture taken with an orphan, or to write a newsletter of our "sacrificial service" is as deep as some ministries go. Driven by this craze to be seen, the Pharisees had little impact on world needs.

When spiritual activity becomes a matter of trying to guarantee one's acceptance with God, there is nothing more enslaving. Persons constantly checking their own righteousness and purity to see if holiness is still perceived leads to a faulty performance-based holiness. The focus settles on rules, regulations, and detailed religious responsibilities deemed necessary to please a holy God. Standards, convictions, and religious activity become the litmus tests for holiness and righteousness. Oneself and others are judged harshly. This mechanical and external preoccupation has been called specializing more in "spiritual dermatology than in spiritual cardiology."[2]

> When spiritual activity becomes a matter of trying to guarantee one's acceptance with God, there is nothing more enslaving.

Jesus reacted against the Pharisees' obstinacy and obsession with outward cleansing over inward purity. He said, "Woe to you, scribes and Pharisees, hypocrites! For you clean the outside of the cup and of the plate, but inside they are full of greed and self-indulgence. You blind Pharisee! First clean the inside of the cup, so that the outside also may become clean" (Matt. 23:25-26). In the mind of God, nothing is clean until first the core is clean. No matter how good we may think we look in our own eyes or in the eyes of others, all of our "good works" amount to nothing in the sight of God if our hearts and motivations are impure.

The Pharisees were so keen on studying the trees (looking at the letters of the law) that they could not find the forest. Jesus condemned this myopic approach to faith that keeps people from the kingdom of God: "But woe to you, scribes and Pharisees, hypocrites! For you lock people out of the kingdom of heaven. For you do not go in yourselves, and when others are going in, you stop them. Woe to you, scribes and Pharisees, hypocrites! For you cross sea and land to make a single convert, and you make the new convert twice as much a child of hell as yourselves" (Matt. 23:13-15).

Because of their loyalty to the outward over the inward, holiness for some Pharisees became more a matter of *cause* than *character*. They became pulpit bullies with a lot of pronouncing and denouncing, but very little announcing about the God of love and grace. Holiness became performance based, a hammer to beat people rather than a message of hope to draw and comfort people. Holiness became a *job* rather than a *joy*.

No wonder Jesus reacted against the Pharisees. They were so different from his Father in heaven. The call of Jesus is to an inward work of personal transformation that produces outward fruit. The quality of the heart will determine the quality of the fruit--not the other way around. If this gets flipped, the whole process will flop.

Driven by the love of law rather than the law of love

The Pharisees emerged in Israel in response to religious, cultural, and political developments extending back to the Greek Empire and perhaps earlier. By the time of Jesus they had become religious leaders in Israel. They had as allies a group of eminent scholars who were zealous for God's Law. As the clergy and religious culture of Judaism moved increasingly in a secular direction, a group of pious laypersons rose up to reclaim the identity of the Jews as people of God's Word. They were determined to get back to the basics of the Hebrew tradition.

Seeing themselves as guardians of the Law, the Pharisees tended to become bigger than the Law, even if inadvertently. Their love of the Law became a tool (sometimes a weapon) in their hands to manage people rather than help people. It was at this point in their history that Jesus came on the scene. He saw religious leaders who had begun to act as masters of the Law that should have been mastering them and determining their character. The end result was low-life "lawyering"—finding loopholes to massage the Law, creating their own rules that occasionally misused the Law, elevating their own traditions in ways that minimized the Law. Driven by their love of law, they had forgotten *the law of love*.

When love of law overshadows the law of love, all kinds of distortions begin to happen. The Pharisees give us some classic examples of the Law gone amuck—not because the Law is bad but because hearts were bad. Here are three of the resulting distortions that bring darkness on the light of life. They were problems of the Pharisees that also have plagued holiness people of more recent times.

Problem #1. It "fences the Law"

In order to keep from breaking the Law, other laws are created around the Law. The problem is that these lesser laws become traditions and convictions of their own that are thought more significant to holiness than the law of love.

Problem #2. It is exacting and exclusive

When the love of law overshadows the law of love, rules trump both redemption and relationships. This is where the Pharisees stumbled most. When Jesus showed the law of love with the woman caught in adultery, the Pharisees saw no room for redemption. The deeper exposure of their own sinful hearts only hardened them the more. They had followed this course to its deepest pit—a rigid positioning of oneself on "holiness" claims without the presence of true heart holiness. Such people, supposedly the most "religious" of all, remain exacting and exclusive and know little of what it means to be kind and caring.

Some years ago, I (Hubert) attended early morning prayer meetings at a holiness camp. The father of a wayward son led out in prayer one morning with a taste of bitterness against the one who had turned his back on "holiness." This poor son was berated before God in a sanctimonious prayer that neither touched heaven nor the son. It was exacting and exclusive in tone. I thought to myself, "No wonder the son turned his back on holiness. In that environment I would have done the same." It was the father who needed true holiness. Then maybe the son would respond.

Problem #3. It divides rather than unites

The Pharisees championed the letter rather than the spirit of the Law. This led to literalism where practices like circumcision became the real thing rather than a picture of the real thing. This thinking was so toxic that Paul straightforwardly dealt with it: "For a person is not a Jew who is one outwardly, nor is true circumcision something external and physical. Rather, a person is a Jew who is one inwardly, and real circumcision is a matter of the heart—it is spiritual and not literal. Such a person receives praise not from others but from God" (Rom. 2: 28-29).

Having participated for a decade in the national dialogue between leaders of the Church of God movement (Anderson) and the Independent Christian Churches/Churches of Christ, I (Barry) wrote about this "radical" tradition in my 1999 *Radical Christianity*. Then, jointly with historian James North, I also wrote about this dialogue in our 1997 *Coming Together in Christ*. Growing out of all this, I led a seminar for Friends pastors that convened at the Quaker seminary, Earlham School of Religion. We reflected together there on the theme "Radical Christianity in a Postmodern World," especially in reference to the future life and witness of Quakerism. We learned that the gospel of Jesus Christ draws believers together with the uniting power of the Spirit of God that then sends united believers into the world as credible witnesses. The different Christian traditions have their places, but never have they the right to divide Christians from each other by their own traditions.

The Holiness Movement of the nineteenth and twentieth centuries at times became muddled in the quagmire of "dots and tittles." This encouraged a spirit of division which was fertile soil for the birth of small "holiness" denominations that sometimes seemed more attentive to "perfectionism" than to "perfect love." Never was this division as strong as when talking about "entire sanctification," especially in relation to whether it is a crisis work or a progressive work. There was the shorter way, the middle way, the longer way, the Keswick way, etc. Rigidities emerged in this maze of theological nuances, and therefore divisions that weakened the holiness witness in general.

Recalling these holiness aberrations is not a call to thoughtless tolerance and compromise of truth for the sake of unity. We are called to speak boldly for what often is not popular but known to be true. Even so, truth announcement cannot be allowed to deteriorate into personal denouncement of sinners. Ours is to be the joy of proclaiming the promises of God for full deliverance from sin in ways that do not castigate hearers. They are to be won to love by love! If we come in the spirit of loving unity, the opportunities for sharing and actually being heard will be greater. All too many holiness preachers have preached themselves into smallness and ineffectiveness by treating people as enemies rather than potential friends.

Tragically, like the Pharisees, too many live and die with sharp lines of spiritual demarcation. They work hard at leaving no margin for error and denouncing anyone who falls short of their standard of measurement. Like the Pharisees, their pronouncements become cold, harsh, and heartless. Jesus had more patience with ignorance than he did with this kind of spirit. He saw the Pharisees for what they often were, saying, "Woe to you, scribes and Pharisees, hypocrites! For you are like whitewashed tombs, which on the outside look beautiful, but inside they are full of the bones of the dead and of all kinds of filth" (Matt. 23:27). Many holiness people need to become recovering Pharisees.

Dark Alleys

The Pharisees make us aware of spiritual blind alleys that can leave us at deadends. But there are other dangers that are common today. Here are five worthy of careful attention.

The dark alley of a holiness without mercy

We spoke above of the harsh judgments of the Pharisee. A broken law often left broken people. I (Hubert) had a conversation with a strong proponent of holiness who had spent most of his life in the academic world. He was a "no nonsense" man who demanded the same of his students and those who worked for him. He was highly regarded for his teaching and preaching abilities and his strong leadership. He stood in line to be the next president of the college he was helping to lead. Then things went wrong. Political maneuvering by the governing board cut him off. He left the school and struggled to find his way. He was betrayed and disillusioned and began struggling with bitterness. It was my privilege to spend time with him that involved honest sharing. With sad eyes, he looked at me and said, "Hubert, the Holiness Movement desperately needs a theology of failure."

A problem many people have with holiness is its seeming intolerance, or at least nervous discomfort with failure. In the minds of some, holiness automatically implies the absence of sin. So, if one does sin, what happens to holiness? Many holiness people have agonized under the yoke of "sinless perfection." The options appear to be redefining sin as a personality disorder or something else, covering it and living in denial or ending the holiness quest altogether. All three options are what we might call "holiness without mercy," dark alleys of unnecessary default and defeat.

God is not a tyrant, quick to cut one off when imperfect performance persists. While sin is always serious, mercy is available. Known sin should be quickly acknowledged and confessed. If we cover it, rename it, or minimize it, we bring great harm to our sense of integrity, the very groundwork for true holiness. John speaks about the readiness of God's grace to forgive: "My little children, I am writing these things to you so that you may not sin. But if anyone does sin, we have an advocate with the Father, Jesus Christ the righteous" (1 Jn. 2:1).

One day when I (Hubert) was in college, I was hurrying to the dining hall from the music building in order to be on time. It was the dead of winter and, although they had de-iced the walkway, there was ice on the grass. As I was passing a group of girls, I slipped on the ice and fell right in front of them. It was an inglorious moment in my life. You can be sure that I was up in an instant to get away from the amusement of these witnesses. Nothing in me said I needed to go back to the music building and start my journey all over again. Everything told me to keep going to my goal, even more rapidly. The same is true when we fall spiritually—not by making sin a practice, but when we fall at any given point. We need to seek the mercy of God *and go on.* There is no need to go back, to cast everything away. Provision has been made for our failures!

One of the great problems that pursuers of holiness face is the harsh judgment of those around them who, in their opposition to holiness as even a possibility, have no mercy with holiness people who fail at any given point. Opposers use failures as persecution. Ironically, while accusing holiness people of occasionally faulty performance, they themselves are actually the ones who are hung up on performance—demanding that any holiness be sinless perfection. They know that by raising the bar high enough, no one can ever claim holiness in this life.

The main problem with sinless-perfection thinking is that it has made sin the main issue. In fact, sin is a by-product of a deeper problem—the problem of imperfect or misplaced love. Was not this Adam and Eve's main problem? They turned their faces away from God to self with all they thought self could have. Paul, when speaking of Demas' departure, said, "for Demas, in love with this present world, has deserted me and gone to Thessalonica" (2 Tim. 4:10). He uses the same Greek word for "love" that is used when speaking of divine love—*agape* love. Instead of a first-preference love for God, Demas had a first-preference kind of love for the world.

The Bible never speaks of sinless perfection but it does speak of perfect love (1 Jn. 2:5; 4:12). Even as Jesus was speaking of being perfect like our Father in heaven is perfect (Matt. 5:48), he was referring to loving like our Father loves—especially in reference to loving our enemies. The interesting thing about "love" is that it goes to motive rather than performance. The remarkable thing about holiness is that it does not make us over-performers. It actually makes us under-performers, with the key word being "rest." We can rest from the tyranny of trying to be important or trying to impress God and people. Our significance is in the love of God, not in what we think we have to do to be significant. Our joy is in the purity and delight of just loving fully and being loved fully, not in what we have to do to achieve and be accepted.

Love certainly affects positively our life performance because love is active and aggressive, but it does not rest there. It rests in love—God's love for us and our love for God. And there is no greater rest than perfect (whole, complete, pure) love. It covers a multitude of failures. This is liberating because, with motive as the qualifier, the actual point of sinning in God's sight depends on motive and not on our performance alone.

Some sinned before the transgression

This is what Jesus was getting at when he spoke of adultery happening when a man looks on a woman to lust after her (Matt. 5:28) or when a man who hates his brother already has the judgment of murder on him (Matt. 5:22). The consummation of the act may not have taken place or may never take place, but the sin has already taken place because it has been embraced in the heart. The Holy Spirit will be faithful to warn and we must be as faithful to deal quickly with a temptation or it will best us.

Some sin at the point of transgression

A person acts negatively as a matter of a twisted nature. When a temptation presents itself, the negative action is almost automatic. This person needs to find the place of surrender to God's Spirit— dying to the sinful self, experiencing the power of God to transform one's very nature and launch a new, a holy walk with God.

Some sin after the transgression

A person may not have thought about it prior, but in a moment of carelessness there is an action quite unbecoming of a Christian. In this case, the Holy Spirit convicts of the sin. If that conviction is resisted, if excuses are made and "reasons" are given, if that wrong is not made right, that person has then entered into sin. If there is sorrow, quick repentance and an asking for forgiveness, the offending person can move on in the way of holiness, now the better for it.

The dark alley of a holiness without wholeness

Just as dangerous as holiness without mercy is holiness without wholeness. The one does not allow for failure, the other allows for almost anything. We must find the biblical balance between these two or end up with a theology that suits everyone but changes no one. The power of the holiness message is its transforming power. It is important for us to avoid soft thinking that can erode the very truth of holiness.

> The center of the holiness message is its transforming power.

The Holy Spirit brings needed and actual change. If certain behaviors are unbecoming, they can be changed if we will allow it. The excuse of "it's just the way I am" is lame from God's point of view. This is the self-centered person's way out of needed cleansing from unnecessary wrongness. Holiness allows for God's remolding of our lives "until we all attain to the unity of the faith, and of the knowledge of the Son of God, to a mature man, to the measure of the stature which belongs to the fullness of Christ" (Eph. 4:13).

It is important to say again that the wholeness that God seeks for us first and foremost is a heart wholeness that aligns our whole spirit and attitude with the ways of God. We are to be "clay in the potter's hands" without anything foreign that resists the clay being remolded. Pure clay is not fully formed clay, but it is clay that is easily formed in God's hands.

My wife and I (Hubert) enjoy the pottery made in many different countries. While in the Cusco area of Peru, we purchased some cherished pieces of pottery designed and molded by Edwardo Seminario, a man famous for the purity and beauty of his pieces. We delighted in it because we knew it was *de calidad*, of quality both in its material and its master. His work is praised widely. Ironically, how often we allow for less when it comes to the Master Potter's work in our hearts and lives.

There is an appalling preference for sin-language these days. Some seem to have a certain pleasure, almost as a badge of honor, in giving testimonies that are permeated with confession of ongoing rebellion, shortcomings and failure, but still laden with a lot of God's grace and love. It is disheartening to hear the words of some newer Christian "pop" songs that are riddled with suggestions of sinfulness and selfishness, as if this were natural and normal in Christian experience. The overriding themes appear to be grace and love in spite of sin, instead of grace that delivers from sin. This kind of language has become common even in Bible studies, becoming the default mode for the absence of victorious Christian living.

The dark alley of a holiness without discipline

A Christian without early and ongoing discipline will struggle with Bible language concerning suffering, sacrificial love, slave/servant, and athlete. These all point to significant discipline required for success in a serious (holy) Christian life. The fact is that anyone who does not enter into proper spiritual disciplines will never know holiness. Discipline is the muscle of holiness and, although it cannot sanctify on its own, it does strengthen the muscles that are vital to the holy life. When discipline is lacking, the "world" is likely to win the day.

I (Hubert) was included in an e-mail roundtable taking place with some Kenyan national leaders and missionaries. The question was why Kenya, like Rwanda, Burundi, and Congo, countries that had been significantly "Christianized," broke out in tragic ethnic fighting and killing. Many of the travesties happened where a holiness denomination was the strongest Christian presence. The response of one national church leader gripped me. He said, "The reason is, we did evangelism without discipleship." We focus so much on getting people saved that we neglect getting saved people into the depths of a matured Christian life.

Reversing this serious neglect should be paramount in all the teaching and preaching of the church. Great harm comes to the church when it lacks the vital disciplines of serious discipling. No amount of saving and sanctifying

> We focus so much on getting people saved that we neglect getting saved people into the depths of a matured Christian life.

grace can make up for it. All is by divine grace, of course, but not without our willing cooperation. Discipline is one of the key colors of holiness.

Holiness makes us easy learners

There is a wonderful characteristic of a child, and it is interesting that Jesus admonished us to become as little children (Matt. 18:3). Though the inference was to their simplicity and humility, one cannot help but note that studies continue to show that formation in a person's life happens mainly up to age twelve—when we are still children. Jewish tradition celebrates a young boy becoming a man at age twelve. If this childhood formation is true, maybe underneath Jesus' words, "except you become as a little child you will in no wise enter the Kingdom of heaven," was an underlying meaning of "don't ever grow up!"—like little children, keep learning and changing. Those who do not learn easily and change easily soon become set in their ways, hard, and difficult, a killer to personal spiritual and church life.

Disciplines of learning take place through purposeful and consistent involvement in Bible reading and study. They should tackle the issues of the day rather than just the personal concerns of the group or individual. Holiness people ought to delve into the difficult areas of illegal immigration, ethnic division, environmental pollution and destruction, to name only a few. They ought to learn how best to bring Jesus to very different and controversial groups of people. This should lead to more intensive and intelligent prayer time.

The discipline of a disciple also should include the reading of quality Christian books, immersing the mind in good Christian biographies and autobiographies, and joining accountability groups. John Wesley gave guidance to small cell groups, encouraging them to ask the following questions of each other:

--What known sins have you committed since our last meeting?

--What temptations have you met with?

--How were you delivered?

--What have you thought, said, or done, of which you doubt

whether it be sin or not?

--Have you nothing you desire to keep secret?

Wesley also encouraged each believer to ask and answer each day questions such as:

--Am I consciously or unconsciously creating the impression that

   I am better --than I am? In other words, am I a hypocrite?

--Am I honest in all my acts and words, or do I exaggerate?

--Do I confidentially pass onto another what was told me in

   confidence?

--Am I a slave to dress, friends, work , or habits?

--Am I self-conscious, self-pitying, or self-justifying?

--Is the Christ-life real in me?

Finally, and always, we must be immersed in regular church life involving preaching, teaching, worship, a small group, and service. Nothing should substitute for one's involvement in a local church. We have no excuse that allows settling for a weak Christianity, immature, ineffective, unholy.

Wesley's practices and call to Christian discipline would make most of us cringe with some of the details. But those disciplines made soldiers out of young believers, turned England upside down, and set on fire the early North American Methodist movement. These were not powder-puff Christians going to a tea party. They were holy people who really knew a holy God. They exercised holiness and produced men and women of spiritual steel. They were Spirit-filled, Spirit-trained Christians on mission. They glowed with the likeness of God and the world had to reckon with them. Our hearts should cry out—Color me holy!

Holiness makes us servants

There is the striking story of Paul and Mark. This young man had felt the sting of Paul's refusal to take him on another missionary trip. Paul's expectations for ministry were high. When Mark did not meet expectations, it caused a division between Paul and Barnabas (Acts 15:36-39). Some years later Paul found himself in prison for the gospel. In writing from there to Timothy, Mark's name came up. Now things had changed. There was a new appreciation of and gratitude for Mark. Paul urges Timothy to bring Mark with him the next time he comes because, reports Paul, "he is useful in my ministry" (2 Tim. 4:11). The word useful literally means "easily used." What powerful words. What a witness to personal transformation!

"Easily used." This is a wonderful description of a holy Christian who is the working bee of church life, the servant going here and there, anywhere and everywhere to find the very stuff that makes the honey of life. Christian work without these dedicated disciples is a work that will languish. Without them we will forever be plagued and hampered with quitters, gripers, and whiners.

In a world that suffers with the poor showing of undisciplined workers—I (Hubert) have asked God to increase the number of missionaries who know what it means to pray, work and serve with all their hearts. There is plenty that will keep undisciplined hearts from the task at hand. I am reminded that "the eyes of the Lord range throughout the entire earth, to strengthen those whose heart is true to him" (2 Ch. 16:9). John Wesley once said, "Give me one hundred preachers who fear nothing but sin and desire nothing but God and I care not a straw whether they be clergymen or laymen, such alone will shake the gates of hell and set up the Kingdom of heaven upon earth." Amy Carmichael (1867-1951) wrote: "We are called to be the Lord's diehards, to whom can be committed any kind of trial of endurance, and who can be counted upon to stand firm whatever happens. Surely fortitude is the sovereign virtue of life... O God, give me fortitude."

The dark alley of a holiness without humility

John Wesley saw pride as the greatest temptation and danger to holiness of heart. He warned strongly against any presence of pride. Anyone who lets this monster creep into preaching, teaching, praying, witnessing, or service has put a huge divide between themselves and God. A person may impress many observers with special skills but stumble over self. Pride cannot be merely suppressed. It will surface again. It can be felt, demanding place and prestige. It can be heard, demeaning people and programs. It can be seen, desiring praise and platitudes. It will come through in some form or another, finally harming relationships and organizations, robbing them of what they could be.

Prideful people, usually excessive with their show of backslapping, look on others as a means to an end rather than people to respect and love. Pastors begin to count the numbers rather than caring about souls. Missionaries begin to count the donors rather than caring about discipleship. Business people begin to count the dollars rather than caring about service. Church members begin to count the people benefits rather than caring about love.

Prince Caspian is a featured character in the *Chronicles of Narnia* by C. S. Lewis. After the decisive battle, the great lion Aslan announces that the prince is now able to assume his rightful kingship.

Caspian, however, expresses uncertainty about whether he is ready to carry such a large responsibility. He is grateful, but humble. Aslan responds with an unexpected reassurance. "It's for that very reason that I know you are!" Humility is a clear mark of Christian maturity, of holy readiness to carry responsibility.

Great harm has come to Christian institutions and churches that started out as bastions of holiness but soon allowed self-importance to dominate the agenda. True holiness is marginalized while other things take precedence. They come to thrive on the things that pride thrives on and proceed with not a clue about what happened to them—not seeing that they are long dead though their structures live on. Pride is always deadly!

The dark alley of a holiness without joy

Any holiness that does not make a joyful people is not holiness. The most colorful people in the world are those on the highway of true holiness, with the sound and sight of pure praise, pure laughter, pure singing, and pure fellowship filling the community. But many have diluted holiness into something giving the impression that lemons are the favorite fruit of the faithful. Paul emphasizes joy in the list of the spiritual fruit of God's Spirit—joy is sandwiched in between love and peace (Gal. 5:23).

> The most colorful people in the world should be those on the highway of true holiness, with the sound and sight of pure praise, pure laughter, pure singing, and pure fellowship filling the community.

The late nineteenth-century Holiness Movement was driven by joy. Meetings were filled with the joy of full salvation. Testimonies were laced with the joy of full cleansing. Singing danced with the joy over God's goodness. How is it that some of these joyful people and settings became known as joy-killers? Sadly, what started out with such enthusiasm often ended up with great restraints. Instead of being known for their fullness of life, holiness people became known for their colorless dress, colorless demeanor, and colorless disciplines, all seemingly intended to keep one from looking too much like the world. That is not holiness that radiates the color of God! Holiness people ought to enjoy the world much more than the world ever can because "this is our Father's world"—and it is good.

Joy bursts throughout the pages of Scripture like geysers that cannot be suppressed. It fills the darkness with singing. When some of the Pharisees told Jesus to quiet the praise of his disciples, Jesus answered, "I tell you, if these were silent, the stones would shout out" (Lk. 19:40). Joy is in the very creation of God because it is the very nature of God. We need to come out of the dark alley of gloom, despair and agony. May God help us to find again the joyful voice of holiness.

As we come to the end of this chapter, we urge you to look for the light of God's glory, to come out of the dark, blind alleys that Satan wants to entrap us. For too long, holiness has been off course. The next two chapters will take us on the ride of our lives—holiness coming back on course. As you take this ride, hear this caution. Do not attempt to live holiness in isolation, trying to hide in some "sacred" place and live only around "good" people in order to protect God's gracious provision. Holiness, while not of this world, belongs very much in this world.

Notes

[1] Percival Wesche, *Henry Clay Morrison: "Crusader Saint"* (reprint, Wilmore, KY: First Fruits Press, 2013), 174.

[2] Tom Hovestol, *Extreme Righteousness* (Authentic Media, 1997), 208.

Holiness.... Back on Course

New Hope

Chapter 6

Inheriting the Brightness

God sacrificed Jesus on the altar of the world to clear that world of sin....
This is not only clear but it's *now*—this is current history! God sets things
right. He also makes it possible for us to live in his rightness. (Romans
3:25-26, *The Message*)

Can anything be clearer or more wonderful than Paul in Romans 3 (above)? God has acted in Jesus to enable forgiveness of our sins. But there is more. That death of Jesus long ago is very much alive right now! Forgiveness is to be followed by something else, something radical, wonderful, and contemporary. God's Spirit is prepared to enable us forgiven sinners, we "righted" ones, to live *in God's rightness*—to be holy today. We are privileged to inherit such reconciliation by God's grace, and then we are responsible to reflect its brightness on our daily lives.

Walking Day by Day

It appears to be such a long road. Many of us are tempted to not even begin the trip. We end the journey to "Christian perfection" at the starting line, not taking the first steps because so many others, probably too many other steps would have to follow. Holiness is an act of God *for us* and must be a day-by-day walk *by us*.

Think about the Christian life with this image of a long road in mind. To live it right, to become all that is envisioned in the Bible for true followers of Jesus is indeed a large challenge. To leave everything and follow the Master into some brave new world is an overwhelming and even frightening prospect. It involves a spiritual journey that few of us are willing to take. The easiest thing to do is nothing.

Some things are very clear. We humans are all weak and imperfect. To begin a spiritual journey with Jesus surely will lead from one major challenge to another, likely from one frustration and failure to another. Who wants to face that? It is a difficult dilemma. On the one hand, we hear the Bible's call to be "holy." On the other hand, no one wants to be put on a pedestal so that the critics can see us and smile at the spectacle?

Still, the fact is that living a vibrant Christian life must involve the holiness journey. We are called to be "saints." God's command and expectation is that we be holy because God is holy. Without holiness we will not see God. What God has done in Jesus is reconcile us "in his fleshly body through death so as to present you holy and blameless and irreproachable before him—provided that you continue securely established by being steadfast in the faith..." (Col. 1:22-23). This journey to "securely established" and "steadfast in the faith" is not easy, and certainly will not be finished with the first few steps. Even so, should we not be running the race rather than sitting in the stands immobilized because we doubt that we could make it to the finish line?

What about risking the first steps? We were not born as adults, so why expect instant holiness just beyond the beginning line? Not starting at all dooms us to failure. If God calls, might not God also provide? If we are going to fail, is it not better to do it while striving for the goal rather than just lying down in our coffins and refusing to breathe until death mercifully comes? As the Wesleyan/Holiness tradition has stressed for many generations, believers are called to "go on to perfection."

Believers can rest assured in this. As we determine to go on, God goes with us as the constant guide and provider. The Greek word *poikilos* might be called the many-colored word of the New Testament. It was used outside Scripture of a leopard's skin, the sheen that glistens off the plumage of some birds, and the multi-faceted glint that radiates off granite when light strikes at just the right angle. One older Bible translation renders *poikilos* as "diverse" and a newer one as "various." Jesus healed diverse diseases--a big range with widely differing manifestations (Matt. 4:24, Mk. 1:34, etc.). There are diverse lusts or various pleasures of the heathen appearing in all revolting colors (Titus 3:3). As we go on toward perfection we will encounter various off-color doctrines (Heb. 13:9). Discoloration will be seen on all hands.

But there also is the positive. Even though journeying believers will have to face various (*poikilos*) trials (1 Pet. 1:6), we are encouraged to believe that we should "consider it nothing but joy, because you know that the testing of your faith produces endurance; and let endurance have its full effect so that you may be mature and complete, lacking in nothing" (James 1:2-4). The most telling biblical use of *poikilos* is in 1 Peter 4:10 where the "manifold" grace of God is highlighted. Here is the dramatically colorful good news. There is no discoloration in sinful lives that cannot be matched by a divine beauty ready to redeem. There is no human situation, from the golden sunshine of joy to the somber grey of pain and sorrow, in which God's grace lacks the corresponding color necessary to bring back light and introduce new hope.

The challenge of holiness is to become "good stewards of the manifold grace of God" by serving each other with "whatever gift each of you has received" (1 Pet. 4:10). The gifts of God are as diverse as the needs of believers, addressing in their totality the full range of salvation and service needs. In the face of this world's garbage dump of rotting colors, God provides a bouquet of saving and equipping beauty. Therefore, we are to walk day by day in faith and confidence realizing that we sinful orphans have been adopted by the all-color God.

We Have Been Adopted!

Kevin and Maria were already blessed with two biological children. Still, they felt led by God to give newness of life to a child born in less fortunate circumstances and with little hope of healthy survival. After all of the waiting and anxiety that comes with adopting from another country, there finally came the day of great family celebration at the Cincinnati, Ohio, airport. The family met and welcomed into their lives this little child from the war-torn, poverty-stricken Democratic Republic of Congo. There is no greater joy than witnessing this kind of happening.

Little did this seven-month-old baby know about what was happening. All of a sudden, a child without hope was surrounded by hope; a child who knew little about love was overwhelmed with love; a child who knew nothing about family was encircled by family; a child without inheritance was given the family name with all its rights and privileges. It was an act of love and grace and new life.

Little Oliver arrived suffering from malnutrition, struggling with malaria, and handicapped with what was soon diagnosed as minor cerebral palsy. One year later, after intense physical therapy to correct leg and arm dysfunctions, Oliver was pronounced completely normal. This healthy little boy is now learning, talking, laughing (and, yes, crying), jumping, climbing, and playing as if nothing had ever been wrong. The adults in the family remember well how wrong things once were, but that had not stopped them from adopting and loving.

The dark fact is that we all have been orphaned from what God intended us to be. However, another fact is much more bright and glorious. We who were mere slaves of sin are now being granted the possible status of *divine family members*! Faith in this promise can flower into an array of amazing new-life colors. Despite all the darkness covering the earth in the twenty-first century, or maybe because of it, there is a hunger for life and love that is reaching out in hope of receiving new life from God. We need and want to be adopted.

The Bible tells the long story about God establishing and sustaining an intimate relationship with dysfunctional people who nonetheless were chosen to be God's own. The Bible is essentially about this story, one of covenant, community making, God's choosing and loving a people. To remember and believe this story leads to claiming our own adoption by God, to really belonging, to understanding the present and embracing the future in light of a defining biblical past. In other words, to activate our adoption by God roots in our embracing as our own the long and blazing glory of God's adoptive history with us wayward humans. This glory exudes the warmth of soft blues and releases the brightness of colorful yellows and reds. They are all colors of God's grace lighting the way to and flowing from new life in Jesus Christ.

When the time was right, at the highpoint of the biblical story, God acted in Jesus. Now, because of this gracious action of God, we are privileged to be "no longer a slave but a child, and if a child then also an heir" (Gal. 4:5, 7). We have been given the power to become children of God because we have been re-born by the will of God (Jn. 1:12-13).

What, then, is Christian holiness? It is really belonging to God's adopted family, being intentionally on the way to faith's adulthood by being wrapped in the welcoming arms of the Holy Spirit. It is love coming into full flower. While we were yet sinners, Christ died for us. We are able to love him now because he first loved us then, called and adopted us so that we can truly belong--to God, to God's people, and—by extending God's love--to God's great work in today's still-dark world.

Believers in Jesus Christ come to belong to a new community of adoptees, the church. This new family relationship comes about because of an actual new birth. By being joined with Jesus, born of his Spirit, we are adopted by God, actually becoming sons and daughters of the Most High. There is a wonderful New Testament word, the Greek *huiothesia*. It literally means "placing as a son." We who did not belong now do belong. We who were mere slaves of sin are granted the status of divine family members as we bow in reverence to the sovereign majesty of the redeeming God.

Our sorrow and repentance over sin can be changed to the cleansing of God's purifying presence. Adopted, changed, commissioned, colored by the brushes of the greatest Artist, holiness is God painting with the oils of his own beauty! The full intention of our spiritual adoption is to bring love, safety, security, health, and wholeness into a desperate child's life. These form the groundwork for love and trust—the strongest link between child and parent.

Surrounding this kind of loving relationship is a wonderful biblical word, the Hebrew *shalom* meaning "peace" or "wholeness." The Greek and Latin words *eirene* and *pax* would have been well known by those living in New Testament times. These were the words Julius Caesar and his successors used when they proclaimed that they had brought peace to the Roman Empire through their conquests and administration. But there was no trust in this kind of peace. It was fraught with forced submission, fear, and oppression that can lead to rebellion—and does so in families as well. When a child grows up in an environment dominated by rigid rules rather than true trust, resentment and rebellion can soon follow.

The Jews would have been more familiar with the Hebrew word *shalom*. It meant much more than the awkward quiet of forced obedience. It was more than the mere absence of conflict. *Shalom* conveyed the sense that everything in life is as it should be because God is lovingly reigning over the creation and children of the divine are gratefully living in accord with God's will and ways. God's holy ones are peace receivers and bringers.

World Gospel Mission is a Christian ministry that has been privileged to partner with the Africa Gospel Church in Kenya in saving the lives of little babies left in dangerous and deplorable places. Together, they have established a center for abandoned babies near Nakuru—a place where these helpless little ones are given a chance at life. Under the watchful and loving care of Christian people who give full attention to them, these babies begin to flourish. They soon are adopted by Christian Kenyan parents. Pictures are taken that show the glow on these young faces. It is one of *shalom!* Everything is as it should be because they now are under the loving, caring, and watchful eyes of parents ("I belong!")—parents who can be trusted.

There is no greater place to be than where we know that God is on the throne and we are under God's constant, loving, watchful care ("we belong!"). This brings a trust that exudes peace. This is the brightness of adoption, the gorgeous glow of divine grace, the breeding ground of holiness. Trust, fully clothed in the warmth of peace, easily moves from gratitude for the Father's help to the greater blessing of sharing the Father's home and holiness. This is a shift from living under the Father's care (physically and materially) to owning the Father's name (the nature and likeness of God).

Note again these amazing words--"no longer a slave but a child, and if a child then also an heir" (Gal. 4:7). This is sheer beauty. John Newton called it "Amazing Grace." C. Bishop spoke of it as "Such

Love." The words of one hymn capture the glory and grandness of our adoption by God:

> That God should love a sinner such as I,
>
> Should yearn to change my sorrow into bliss,
>
> Nor rest till He had planned to bring me nigh,
>
> How wonderful is love like this!
>
> And now He takes me to His heart—a son;
>
> He asks me not to fill a servant's place.
>
> The "far off country" wanderings all are done;
>
> Wide open are His arms of grace.[1]

God is saying, "All that is mine is yours!" We are heirs together with Christ. Therefore, all that is Christ's is ours. "For you know the generous act of our Lord Jesus Christ, that though he was rich, yet for your sakes he became poor, so that by his poverty you might become rich" (2 Cor. 8:9).

Although there is no doubt that our inheritance includes heaven, with all that heaven means, we have suffered too long at the hands of those who are so heavenly minded that they push everything God has promised spiritually for *this life* to "the sweet by and by." At the other extreme, of course, are those who preach a "prosperity gospel" that tries to bring heaven to earth, not because they want God's will to be done on earth as it is in heaven, but because they want God's wealth to be theirs on earth now as it will be in heaven later.

Above all, our spiritual inheritance is to be enjoyed in this life before it will ever be enjoyed in the next life. We are to be "rich toward God" now (Luke 12:16). This has to do with a relationship in which we are entirely committed to God in all ways and at all times. Anyone who is rich toward God wants nothing less and always looks for even more because he or she revels in the fullness of this joy. It is like true marriage. One who enters it does so with a deep sense of love, intending complete faithfulness, desiring complete purity. This commitment and anticipation form the basis of the joy of the relationship. Why do we expect anything less in our love relationship with God?

When any relationship becomes about what we can get from someone rather than the sheer pleasure of sharing and giving, that relationship has lost the only true color that can give it depth and fulfillment. The story of the Prodigal Son is a classic Jewish story with an interesting twist and a great truth. The twist is in the concept of grace that would return to a prodigal the full blessings of sonship. Another great truth involves the other son who never left home. Sonship without the underpinnings of deep relationship—one gracefully rich toward the father and wayward younger brother—is as bad as being the prodigal. Being Christian in the fullest sense of what God intends and provides is the only basis of true adoption and the resulting abundant life. The redeemed ones become themselves redemptive, the son like the Father.

Recall the older brother of the prodigal who spoke sharply to the father: "Listen! For all these years I have been working like a slave for you, and I have never disobeyed your command; yet you have never given me even a young goat so that I might celebrate with my friends" (Lk. 15:29). Therein lays the tragedy of the church that is full of immature, unholy believers. Like that brother of the prodigal, we live below the privileges of sonship. Replied the father, "'Son, you are always with me, and all that is mine is yours" (Lk. 15:31). This older brother had missed it. He was playing a game, the business of mere religion (doing=getting). He knew nothing about the true relationship of a profoundly grateful adoptee (receiving=giving, delight=dancing). The life of grace found by the younger son is the ground for also finding high-definition holiness—life lost, life received again, a new path of purifying joy provided by the Father.

Preference Satisfaction

The older brother in the story of the prodigal son had thought and sought at a level lower than holiness. We often settle for lesser things and are satisfied with our selfish grabbing and hollow victories. This has been called "preference satisfaction."[2] What I prefer satisfies me. Such an attitude is the sickness of premature satisfaction.

In light of the glorious riches of God's person resident fully in the Father, Son, and Holy Spirit, this kind of low-level satisfaction is unworthy of God's people and is the bane of church life. Jesus observed some religious leaders pridefully performing their prayers in public, drawing admiration for their pious practice. They were getting their reward, the respectful attention of the crowd. But Jesus offered a sharp judgment on these "hypocrites"—simply, "they have received their reward" (Matt. 6:2), the crowd attention being all of it. There would be much more if only they were selfless and sincere.

Luke records a fascinating interaction between Jesus and someone who made himself heard above a pressing crowd (Lk. 12:1). Completely unaffected and clueless as to the rich truths that Jesus was teaching, this man raised his voice with only one thing on his mind. "Teacher, tell my brother to divide the family inheritance with me" (Lk. 12:13). This sounds reasonable to those who seek "preference satisfaction," but Jesus reacted by saying, "who set me to be a judge or arbitrator over you? ...Take care! Be on your guard against all kinds of greed; for one's life does not consist in the abundance of possessions" (Lk. 12:14-15). How often we put God in the role of mediator of our wants, moving him from our *sanctifier* to our *supplier*. This cheapens our relationship with God and impoverishes us spiritually.

What some consider God's answer to their prayers, attainment of material blessings and a sense of satisfaction emotionally, may be nothing more than a testimony to the fact that, like a spoiled child, "I got my way." Sadly, we betray the godlessness, arrogance, and deception of our hearts and culture by such selfishness. Worse yet, we imply that we arranged for God to do it our way—as if that were possible.[3]

There is something very wrong with the picture of our being made for God and settling for "my way!" When the Israelites began to "crave intensely in the wilderness," accusing God of robbing them of Egyptian delicacies, "He gave them what they asked, but sent a wasting disease among them" (Ps. 106:15). One translation says, "He sent leanness into their souls." There are times when we may come out with a win as far as we are concerned in our own selfishness, but our win is the kind that destroys character, integrity, and inner well being. It flies in the face of holiness!

At any point where our preferences take precedence over the higher thinking, culture, and values of the kingdom of God, we strike at the very heart of God's will and reign in creation. We have traded light for darkness by insisting that "my will be done on earth, and my preferences be satisfied on earth." We need a holy revolt (like the prodigal son) against the pig food we have tried to live on. We need a vision and desire for the bright, rich colors of the divine inheritance that still awaits our full surrender and return home to the Father.

The Rich Colors of Our Inheritance

When it comes to spiritual inheritance, what should disturb us most is both what many Christians are seeking and what they are not seeking. An enlightening incident is when Jesus was baptized in the River Jordan by John the Baptist. Matthew records that "as [Jesus] came up from the water, suddenly the heavens were opened to him and he saw the Spirit of God descending like a dove and alighting on him. And a voice from heaven said, 'This is my Son, the Beloved, with whom I am well pleased'" (Matt. 3:16-17).   Beautiful! The pronouncement from the Father God, "This is my Son," was in the context of the Spirit of God descending on Jesus. Knowing and claiming one's divine relatedness is the preface to being filled with God's presence.

The baptism of Jesus was not personally redemptive (Jesus had no sin). His baptism with the Holy Spirit was not personally transforming (Jesus required no change). The event was heavily symbolic of what we need most, and what we should desire and seek above everything else. By this public act, Jesus confirmed that baptism signifies entrance into the family of God and that, as children of God, we can have the fullness of the Holy Spirit in our lives. The Spirit's presence surpasses all else that we stand to inherit. We seek not the "gifts" of the Spirit, but the Gift of the Spirit. When the Spirit comes, so do the divine gifts of service that we need for our kingdom responsibilities.

Many Christians are pleased at the prospect of joining a church crowd at the river and sharing the excitement of some dramatic vision from the sky—as long as it does not demand a life change on their part, a receiving of the Holy Spirit who expects and enables a holy life in the Spirit. Disturbed by the "forgotten God" (the Holy Spirit), Francis Chan writes: "The benchmark of success in church services has become more about attendance than the movement of the Holy Spirit. The 'entertainment' model of church was largely adopted in the 1980s and '90s and, while it alleviated some of our boredom for a couple of hours a week, it filled our churches with self-focused consumers rather than self-sacrificing servants attuned to the Holy Spirit."[4]

Not so with Jesus and the early disciples. As Jesus began to brush the great colors of the Holy Spirit's brightness onto the minds and hearts of those first followers, he succeeded in establishing this question as basic for the church: "Did you receive the Holy Spirit?" (Acts 19:2). Receiving the Spirit was to be their very life, new life radiating divine colors. The Apostle Paul speaks of the "the fruit of the Spirit" (Gal. 5:22-23) as our primary adornment—the bright, rich colors of our spiritual inheritance in Jesus Christ and our preparation for Christian service.

We tend to think of this divine fruit as out-growths or add-ons to our Christian lives, as if with some effort on our part we could pick them up along the way. Without doubt, acquiring spiritual fruit necessitates our involvement—for God does nothing in us if we fail to cooperate. But the beauty about spiritual fruit is that, if it is to have integrity, it will be part of something bigger than itself. It is connected to a particular type of tree with its own root system, food system, and growth system. The roots reach to the very heart of God.

The fruit of the Holy Spirit is like the fruit of an orange tree that by its very nature produces oranges. It cannot because of its nature produce anything other than oranges. The Holy Spirit is holy and produces holy fruit because that is who the Spirit is. This is not fruit to be picked according to our likes or dislikes. We either have the fruit of the Spirit as a whole or none at all because this is who the Holy Spirit is at all times—and who we are to become in the Spirit.

People who know multiple languages frequently are asked to do interpreting and have been frustrated trying to find the right word to capture fully what the other language is saying. This is like Paul struggling for a Greek word to describe the fruit (singular) of the Spirit. He describes it as a love-joy-peace-patience-kindness-goodness-faithflness-gentlenes-self-control kind of fruit (Gal. 5:22). He is not giving us a list of various fruits from which we may pick as we choose. Rather, "he is giving us a list of words that circle around the one character of a Spirit-filled life he is trying to describe."5

The fruit of the Spirit, when actively present in our lives, necessarily exhibits the nature of the divine holiness of God. Again, holiness is a many-splendored thing but can never appear selectively in our lives—where we might have love but not joy, etc. Like the rainbow, the full range of colors would not make a rainbow when any color is absent from the whole. The fruit of the Spirit, like the rainbow, is the fullness of the radiance of God's glory. The Spirit is a kaleidoscope of colors, love colors, joy colors, peace colors, etc.

What God is saying to us is simple and critical. It is that this colorful list is the natural radiance of the very nature of God and that "all that is mine is yours!" We should never forget what Peter says. We should be actual partakers of this amazing nature since "by his [God's] great mercy he has given us a new birth into a living hope through the resurrection of Jesus Christ from the dead, and into an inheritance that is imperishable, undefiled, and unfading" (1 Pet. 1:3-4).

If we will submit to the Spirit's guidance and flow with the Spirit's movement, if we will live by the Spirit (Gal. 5:25), we will come to express the Spirit's life in our own. The Holy Spirit in us, as the very root, source, and fountain of our lives, will burst forth in colorful, delicious fruit shining like sparkling emeralds in our lives, bearing the very nature of God in us. We invite you to take a good look at this fruit of the Spirit. Who has not wished for such fruit in their marriages, in their families, among their friends, in their places of work, and in their dealings with organizations, businesses, and government?

What would the world be like if God's people were full of the fruit of the Spirit and active in all the important places of society, bearing and sharing this fruit? The world longs for this kind of people whether it knows it or not. Every day we put up with behavior and attitudes that are demanding, demeaning, deplorable, and even devastating. God is saying to us, You can show the world a difference; you are to be my heart to them at all times, no matter the circumstances and no matter how you are treated. Jesus put it this way: "I am the vine, and my Father is the vinegrower.... If you abide in me... you bear much fruit and become my disciples" (Jn. 15:1, 7-8).

As we consider the fruit of the Spirit, does it make you hungry for the Spirit kind of life? Take and eat. God has said, "All that is mine is yours!" In a world darkened by fruit that is rotten, people are hungry for someone who is all that God said one can be. Our most urgent prayer, for our sake and the sake of the world around us, should be, God's kingdom come, God's will be done *on earth* as it is in heaven. May God's kingdom come now, and in part through our reflecting the rich colors of our divine inheritance.

The Menu of Heaven

What is God's family all about? If we are inheritors of the divine kingdom through the indwelling presence of God's Spirit, what responsibility do we inherit? We know that it has to do with God's will being done on earth as it is in heaven. But this raises the practical question: How is God's will to be done on earth?

> Certainly it would be done *knowingly.*
>
> No one can deny that it would be done *voluntarily.*
>
> Without a doubt it would be done *immediately.*
>
> There is no question that it would be done *joyfully.*
>
> Who would argue but that it would be done *fully*?
>
> And, given God's gentle Spirit, it would be done *tastefully.*

As with any fruit, the fruit of the Spirit is not just for display and enjoyment (although it is pleasing to the eyes and heart); it is primarily for nourishment and sharing. Not only is the divine fruit health to our own souls but, as we bear this fruit faithfully in the traffic of life, it becomes the source of health for the worlds in which we live, work, and play. Not only is this fruit a deep satisfaction and delight to our own souls, but an amazement to others who have opportunity to taste and see that it is truly good.

> Not only is the divine fruit health to our own souls but, as we bear this fruit faithfully in the traffic of life, it becomes the source of health for the worlds in which we live, work, and play.

Christians should taste good! Kindness, like the full, delicious, meat in a sandwich, is right in the middle of the listed fruit of the Spirit. Who would deny that there is nothing tastier than kindness? But too many Christians are just plain mean in their ways with one another, and too often this negativity spills out on those outside the church. There is nothing more damaging to the Christian cause. The Apostle Paul reminded the church at Galatia of the primacy of the love of neighbor. He warned that "if...you bite and devour one another, take care that you are not consumed by one another" (Gal. 5:15).

Whereas kindness is the meat in the holy sandwich of Christian living, love and self-control are the slices of bread that hold the sandwich together. Inside are other tasteful ingredients, like the very best of joy, peace, patience, generosity, faithfulness, and gentleness. The result surpasses anything available in any human restaurant. This is the menu of heaven, and every child of God ought to be enjoying such a rich and colorful feast.

It needs to be said clearly and repeatedly. There is nothing more damaging to the spread of the gospel of Christ than so-called Christians who act in ways contrary to the fruit of the Spirit. I (Hubert) have the wonderful responsibility of assisting missionaries in fulfilling what they feel is the call of God on their lives. My greatest concern is that we send only those who know the holiness of God in the fullness of the Holy Spirit, the fire of the Holy Spirit, the focus of the Holy Spirit, and the fruit of the Holy Spirit. I (Barry) have been an educator of Christian leaders for decades and have carried exactly the same concern about faculty and students alike.

It is impossible to bear the divine fruit consistently and convincingly without the purifying and powerful presence of the Holy Spirit. The world into which missionaries and pastors and teachers go suffers under the presence of sin and the harmful ways of sinners.

Christian leaders must display a different color and have a different taste, bringing glory and honor to the Father.

The Family Honor

Whereas our most urgent prayer should be that God's "kingdom come, your will be done on earth as it is in heaven," the prayer must be based on "our Father in heaven, hallowed be your name." Being a member of the holy family of God involves concern for family honor. The concept of holiness, as the children of Israel came to grasp it, was honed in the Middle Eastern culture of honor and shame which looks at things differently than our current culture of guilt and innocence. The Jews (the Bible) understood honor in ways we sometimes struggle to grasp.

God can be more "Middle Eastern" than "Western" in some ways. From God's point of view, events and people trump time. The same is true about relationships. People always are to be valued more than the clock and calendar. If Christians want to succeed in today's secularized world, they must learn to appreciate the people and the events that matter to them. While Americans look nervously at their watches and smart phones, other cultures give more full and relaxed attention to the person.

And so it is in the matter of honor and shame. In biblical culture, dating back to Adam and Abraham and on through both the Old and New Testament periods, honor was a huge issue. Therefore, it is impossible to ignore this highly valued sense of honor in the whole concept of holiness. To be holy involves honoring a name and a community.

Holiness Honors a Name

The Bible is replete with honor language and overtones. Note just a few:

> Leviticus 22:2. "Direct Aaron and his sons to deal carefully with the sacred donations of the people of Israel, which they dedicate to me, so that they may not profane my holy name; I am the Lord."

> Psalm 103:1. "Bless the Lord, O my soul, and all that is within me, bless his holy name."

> Isaiah 29:23. "For when he sees his children, the work of my hands, in his midst, they will sanctify my name; they will sanctify the Holy One of Jacob, and will stand in awe of the God of Israel."

Luke 1:49. "for the Mighty One has done great things for me, and holy is his name."

And, of course, the Lord's Prayer directs that we pray: "Our Father in heaven, hallowed by your name" (Matt. 6:9).[6]

When fully clothed in the warmth of peace, trust easily moves from gratitude for the Father's help to the greater blessing of sharing the Father's home and holiness.

When Jesus responded to his disciples' request to teach them how to pray, he took hold of that longstanding divine brush and painted the perfect picture of humble honoring.

"Pray then in this way: 'Our Father in heaven, hallowed be your name.'" Stop and look at this picture. Jesus boldly splashes across the canvas the brightest color that is to be seen. Holy be God's name! This color is not just something to declare by acknowledging God as holy with our words. Anyone can do that. This color is something to *demonstrate*. The word "hallowed" is in the active voice, meaning that by our very lives we are to hallow, sanctify, or make God's name known as holy. And only hearts that have been touched with the brush and colors of God's holiness can honor a holy God in this high and holy way.

There is a descriptive Spanish response often used with a child who is misbehaving. Someone will point a finger at the child and say, "*Mal criado!*" Literally, this means "raised bad." The interesting thing is that this response focuses on the parents more than the child. The child is demeaning the parents with his or her poor life testimony. How often this is done with God's name. Sometimes people refuse to attend church because of the bad behavior of someone in the church—God's name has been dishonored. On the other hand, a child can bring honor to the parent with good behavior. This is carried in the command to "honor your father and your mother." As with child and parents, our lives should speak well of God—bringing honor to the divine name by our lives—in word and deed.

The greatest gift a parent can give to children is to build into them this sense of honor, not by force, but through true respect that has been earned in daily love and discipline so essential in a child's life. This makes it much easier when the time comes for that child to respond to the voice of God with a sense of honor. A child who has not been given these basic ingredients for true honor, or who has been allowed to get away with attitudes of self-centered rebellion toward authority, will be more likely to struggle with submission to God's ways.

Could poor parenting be the reason for the increasingly cocky and disrespectful attitudes toward spiritual values so prevalent these days? Could this be one reason for the debilitating self-will and lack of discipline that dominate much of Christian experience, even among those who consider themselves good and responsible Christians? George Barna draws a disturbing conclusion from his considerable research:

> Literally tens of millions of American Christians have denied God His rightful place on the throne of our lives and withheld control of our lives so that we, not He, can reign supreme, all under the cover of being "good and responsible Christians." You and I have convinced ourselves that our inability to...give God total control of all aspects of our lives is a natural and common failing, a weakness that is both predictable and expected...despite all the self-recommending activities we list or the theological truths we know and intellectually believe....[7]

What Jesus is teaching in the first part of the Lord's Prayer is that the results of Barna's research should not and need not be as they are. The world ought to be able to look at a Christian's life and be encouraged to glorify the Father. This goes to the very heart of what Jesus was saying when he declared, "You are the light of the world. Let your light shine before others so that they may see your good works and give glory to your Father in heaven" (Matt. 5:14-16). Our "predictable weakness" need not be the last word. The numerous sex scandals involving Roman Catholic priests present a devastating anti-witness to the world. Protestants, unfortunately, often have not done much better.

Light! There is available the glorious light of God's holiness. There is nothing more attractive than to carry the divine colors with honor—bringing honor/glory/blessing to God! How can we, while claiming to be God's children, be satisfied with dishonoring God by bad behavior, daring to do so by default but still "in his name"? There is a poison mixed in the pot of much contemporary theology—a poison as old as what came from the serpent in the Garden of Eden. It makes us think we can sin and not die, that we can repent and not change, that we can bear bad and good fruit at the same time and still bring glory to God. This is an appalling contradiction to the underlying meaning of "Hallowed be Your name." It is walking with backs turned to the highway of holiness.

Remember that Paul says, "For we are His [God's] workmanship, created in Christ Jesus to do good works, which God prepared in advance for us to do" (Eph. 2:10, NASB). God likes to display his handiwork, knowing when something is "very good" and worth seeing (Gen. 1:31). God goes beyond condemning a fallen world; God determines that through the Spirit-life of his people the world can be enabled at least to glimpse the divine glory, a redeeming glory that is lovingly available for all. Here is a beautiful translation of some important words of Jesus to his disciples: "You're here to be light, bringing out the *God-colors* in the world. He is a master painter and he delights in pulling the covering off so all can see.... God is not a secret to be kept. We're going public with this, as public as a city on a hill. If I make you light-bearers, you don't think I'm going to hide you under a bucket, do you? I'm putting you on a light stand" (Matt. 5:14-16, *The Message*).

Frankly, if God had not been keen on bringing up one of his best "paintings," Job would have been just fine. Everything was going his way, not because he was doing it "my way," but because he was doing it all God's way. But, as it happened, when Satan appeared before God, God brought up Job's name saying, "Have you considered my servant Job? There is no one like him on the earth, a blameless and upright man who fears God and turns away from evil" (Job 1:8).

These are amazing words! Job was announced to be a holy poem reflecting the beauty of the divine. Satan, however, was convinced that no man could be holy, especially under pressure. So he retorted to God with diabolical intent, "But stretch out your hand now, and touch all that he has, and he will curse you to your face" (Job 1:11). All hell soon broke loose in Job's life, and things got even worse when Job did not capitulate to Satan's designs.

After devastating losses, God again brings Job's name to Satan's attention. Like a proud father "bragging" on his child, God restated Job's uprightness (Job 2:3). This provoked Satan to no end. He would not stand by and let one man dismantle the lie he had created in the minds of men and women—that no one can be righteous or pure (Job 4:17). Who best to destroy Job's claim to holiness than his "friends." They took up this war against Job's purity and integrity, accusing, blaming, and belittling with endless arguments. Even so, "in all this Job did not sin against God." He made his defense, saying, "But [God] knows the way that I take; when he has tested me, I shall come out like gold. My foot has held fast to his steps; I have kept his way and have not turned aside" (Job 23:10-11).

God never accused Job of sin, dealing with him only about his misunderstanding of some large matters—holiness, of course, is not full understanding. When it came to affirmation of Job's purity, God had Job offer a sacrifice *for his troublesome friends*. This was holiness acted out in all its splendor, beauty, and color, bursting out in rays of self-less honor! Finally, there was the overwhelming evidence of *shalom*—all is as it should be because God is humbly acknowledged as on the divine throne.

Job's purity and love is the essence of what Apostle John is getting at in 1 John—that sin and a relationship with God are totally at odds with each other. Indeed, "whoever says 'I abide in him' ought to walk just as he [Jesus] walked" (1 Jn. 2:6). John had no patience with those who prattle on about Jesus without taking on the nature of Jesus. "If we say that we have fellowship with him while we are walking in darkness, we lie and do not do what is true" (1:6). The fact is that "those who are born of God do not sin" (5:18).

I (Hubert) had the privilege of doing some graduate work at the Institute of Holy Land Studies (now Jerusalem University College) in Jerusalem, Israel. There were groups of students from Christian colleges who visited for a week or month at a time. I was invited by one of these groups to participate in a study of 1 John. As we studied John's thoughts on holiness, one young man, troubled by what John was saying, finally spoke what many were feeling. He said, "This isn't what I've been taught." The study was finally given up because of "confusion." It contradicted what they had been taught all of their lives. Tragic! Such a beautiful letter, full of promise and possibility, and so many either ignore, marginalize, or reinterpret it. This "hallowed be your name" teaching should not be a burden, but a privilege.

Holiness Honors a Community

Community is a difficult subject in our current culture where independence is so highly valued. But community plays a vital part in biblical revelation and culture. To sin against God is to sin against the community of God, and a man like Achan (Gen. 7) paid a heavy price and caused the community to pay a heavy price for his anti-group action. Community holiness was also a vital part of New Testament thinking. No believer is to be independent of the community of faith, and all are to honor the community with constructive attitudes and acts.

This is especially seen in Paul's writing to the church at Corinth. A truth we now tend to personalize is 1 Corinthians 3:16: "Do you not know that you are God's temple and that God's Spirit dwells in you?" We do the same with 1 Corinthians 6:18-20: "Shun fornication! Every sin that a person commits is outside the body; but the fornicator sins against the body itself. Or do you not know that your body is a temple of the Holy Spirit within you, which you have from God, and that you are not your own? For you were bought with a price; therefore glorify God in your body."

These words of Paul to the church at Corinth were written with the use of the *plural* (not singular) pronoun. In other words, they were not written to emphasize individuality but *the body of believers.* Paul was emphasizing that the church is to be God's holy sanctuary, and this community has the responsibility of protecting itself by disciplining the impure member for the sake of that member and the well being of the whole. Paul's view, in effect, was, think body, people. Think body. Honor the body. He believed in corporate holiness as a testimony to the world of Christian unity, love, and purity. He taught that the church protects its body by judging its members (5-6), reigning in its members (8-10), calling for order among its members (11-14), and reminding its members (15-16).

Jesus saw the crowds as "distressed and dispirited" (Matt. 9:36, NASB). He knew that he had to send into the world workers who would be a different kind of community—one not centered on "me" but on "others"—Christians willing to "do nothing from selfish ambition or conceit, but in humility regard others as better than yourselves.... Let the same mind be in you that was in Christ Jesus..." (Phil. 2:3-5). This is radical. Holiness always is. And this takes a radical work of God in the soul. Holiness always does. It creates a new humanity—a new community—a people who are not introverted (into self) but extroverted (all about others). Holiness inspires and embraces a true rainbow of humanity, where color, tribe, race, and culture are all featured but never allowed to be a divisive factor (in fact, they are mutually enriching). This is the high calling of the church. Holiness is the very heart of this calling—bringing a huge soul shift from *me* to *we.* And it will take the "we," working in harmony with each other and God, to get

> Holiness inspires and embraces a true rainbow of humanity where color, tribe, race, and culture are all featured-- but never allowed to be a divisive factor.

the job done. Only the holiness of God in the soul of Christian community can do that. This is the highest honor because it honors God and Christ's bride—the church.[8]

A small congregation in central Indiana always enjoyed its monthly Sunday talent night. It gave everyone a chance to come "out of the closet" with varied abilities and gifts, making everyone feel a part of the whole. On one particular talent night, a young high school girl went to the platform with her trombone. She explained that she was going to be playing a part that she played in the school band. This is where it got interesting. As she played, she would regularly stop, tap her foot for several seconds, toot two or three more notes, then stop and tap her foot again. This went on and on, mostly tapping her foot as her part rested and the remainder of the band played (if it had been there).

Too say the least, this "performance" looked and sounded strange, and soon it became humorous to the congregation. No one wanted to embarrass the young lady, but laughing could not be helped. This is the way any of us would look and sound when separated from the whole to which we naturally belong. It cannot be stated strongly enough. Personal spirituality, going it alone by choice, is "nothing more than new-age paganism unless it is related to the body of Christ. If it is not, it may be great spirituality, but it will never be Christianity."[9]

The church today should be all about community honor. If we have the hope of heaven for later, we should have in heart and mind the honor of today's bride of Christ—the church. This is straightforward: "Heaven is not about you or me individually but about us collectively.... Individualism and heaven are incompatible.... Heaven is not a place where your wildest dreams of personal fulfillment come true—such as landing a fish on every cast or playing video games and always winning. These are pagan notions of heaven. Heaven is about becoming a people. Heaven will melt our stubborn individuality and merge us together into a group—the bride of Christ. It will be the church that goes to heaven, not just a bunch of individual believers. That is why people who reject the church cannot be Christian. They won't melt. They won't join the bride."[10] Personal holiness cannot be fully realized in isolation. It should not be disconnected from the body—the church.[11]

John Wesley was one who strongly believed in the protection of members through body life. He pioneered what some now call "accountability groups." The power of such groups to encourage individual faith and enhance the integrity of the whole community is credited by many as a key reason that the influence of Wesley and his movement continued to grow generations after his death. The genius of Wesley's organization of seekers and young believers, his model for "making disciples" within the larger body of the church is a key missing piece in most congregations today.[12] Paul instructed that we "love one another with mutual affection; outdo one another in showing honor" (Rom. 12:10). This is the deepest meaning of *agape* love—honoring others as a reflection of God's choice to honor us.

The One who "chose us in Christ before the foundation of the world to be holy and blameless before him in love" (Eph. 1:4) is redeeming our rights of ancestry by making us sons and daughters of God *and of each other*. God says, "All that is mine is yours—for your *mutual* benefit." We who have been "born again" have been reborn into a faith family. We are to glory in the grand adoption, inherit and nourish the brightness, and do it *together!*

There is too much pessimism in the Christian community. People hear regularly from the pulpit that Christ commands each believer to love God and others in the way and to the extent that God loves us—unconditionally and sacrificially. Following this hearing, however, often come these questions. Is that possible to do? Was Jesus overstating the situation? Aren't we only sinful humans? Yes, we are sinful; yes, on our own we are quite unable to live the life called for by the Christ; and yes, *holiness is nevertheless possible!*

Dennis Kinlaw recently expressed his gratitude for John Wesley making clear something very important. God's commands are also God's *implicit promises*. "If God tells me to have a pure heart, it is because he has the power to purify my heart. If he tells me to live above conscious sin, it means he can keep me there; he will enable me not to sin. His commands are promises that he will do in me all that I need him to do. His commands are not burdens, but *invitations to freedom.*"[13]

Notes

[1] C. Bishop, "Such Love" in *Worship in Song* (Lillenas Publishing, 1972), 220.

[2] Term coined by Kevin J. Brown, Assistant Professor of Finance at Anderson University, Anderson, Indiana. Now teaches at Asbury University.

[3] Recall the song "I Did It My Way!" composed by Paul Anka and popularized by Frank Sinatra, Elvis Presley, and others.

[4] Francis Chan, *Forgotten God: Reversing Our Tragic Neglect of the Holy Spirit* (David C. Cook, 2009), 15-16.

[5] E. Randolph Richards and Brandon J. O'Brien, *Misreading Scripture with Western Eyes* (InerVarsity Press, Downers Grove, IL, 2012), 74-75.

[6] For a contemporary commentary on the Lord's Prayer, see Barry L. Callen, *The Prayer of Holiness-Hungry People: A Disciple's Guide to the Lord's Prayer* (Francis Asbury Press, 2011), especially pages 31-48.

[7] George Barna, *Maximum Faith* (Metaformation, Inc., 2011), xiiv.

[8] See Steve DeNeff and David Drury, *Soul Shift: Outcomes of a Life Transformed by Christ* (Wesleyan Publishing House, Indianapolis, Indiana 45250, 2011), 125.

[9] Keith Drury, *There is No "I" in Church: Moving Beyond Individual Spirituality to Experience God's Power in the Church* (Wesleyan Publishing House, 2006), 22.

[10] Ibid., 16.

[11] This point is elaborated well by Steve DeNeff and David Drury, *SoulShift*, 125-140.

[12] See D. Michael Henderson, *John Wesley's Class Meeting: A Model for Making Disciples* (Evangel Publishing House, 1997).

[13] Dennis F. Kinlaw, *Prayer: Bearing the World as Jesus Did* (Francis Asbury Press, 2012), 43. Emphasis added.

Chapter 7

Holiness Shines Again!

The Scripture clearly teaches that holiness of heart and life is not only possible in this life but necessary, and it is made possible by the grace of God for all who respond by faith to this clear call of God. The churches of today need this response for their own integrity and growth. It is happening—even if slowly and partially—to God's glory!

We have raised high the banner of Christian holiness in preceding chapters. What we have learned is that holiness, rather than being marginalized in Scripture, is front and center throughout. In this last chapter, we hope to show that holiness can, increasingly is, and must get back on course in today's church. Correct biblical understanding is vital and informed theological awareness in highly desirable. Even so, a heart and life transformed into holiness is fundamental whatever the maturity or education of a believer.

Our prayer is that this final chapter will help us believe again, cause us to hope again, encourage us to seek again, inspire us to trust and look up again to see the rainbow of God's holiness. Holiness can shine again in our lives and bring life back into our churches.

We know that the church's road is rough and traffic is still moving in all directions at once. Holiness language has become quite popular again, just like "spirituality" is in vogue in the culture. A driving force has been the devastating moral and ethical failures of several prominent Christian leaders in the last several years who have pushed this subject to the forefront of public concern, even public scorn. We hear more in the mass media about priests violating young boys than we do about humble believers living selflessly for the good of others. Holiness must shine again!

Sin Is Unacceptable

It is alarming to realize how friendly Christians have gotten with sin. Until there is a deep repugnancy and revolt against its presence in our lives, we will continue to live on a lower plain. When "our bodies are regarded as mere instruments of our autonomous rational wills, repugnance may be the only voice left that speaks up to defend the central core of our humanity. Shallow are the souls that have forgotten how to shudder."[1]

No one would deny that we would be much better off if true holiness ruled the land. We are all uncomfortable by the reality of sin among the "saints." Most sensible Christians know that it should not be this way, so we try to counter with a dose of lectures and literature on how to be more holy in our Christian walk. This is commendable because at least it speaks to the bad taste that un-holiness is leaving in our mouths. True holiness must be a matter of actual character change, a work of divine grace in our hearts, or it will not make the needed difference.

N. T. Wright refers to the need for "the clear through" aspect of character, the pattern of thinking and acting that runs right through someone, like the name that goes right through a stick of Brighton Rock. No matter how much you eat into this stick of English candy, you can still see the name because it runs clear through the stick.[2] You find this same idea in the thinking of the Apostle Paul: "Now may the God of peace himself sanctify you [make you holy] entirely" (1 Thess. 5:23), literally, "through and through." That sounds like something that would affect character significantly.

Holiness is definitely a matter of the heart and of our very characters. And therein lies the heart of the matter. Jesus made this point very clear when he said, "Out of the abundance of the heart the mouth speaks" (Matt. 12:34) and "those things which proceed out of the mouth come from the heart...for out of the heart proceed evil thoughts, murders, adulteries, fornications, thefts, false witness, and blasphemies" (Matt. 15:18,19). This revolutionary thinking is found in both Old and New Testaments. Biblical writers consistently underscore it as right thinking. If holiness is not a matter of the heart, the results will eventually be unholy actions and attitudes, the very things we decry in our church ranks today.

It is disheartening to listen to theologians and want-to-be theologians decry bad living, even making a case for the need for holy living, and in the same breat speak of "sinning saints" as something inevitable and thus acceptable. We have convinced ourselves of our inability, even with God's assisting grace, to give God total control of all aspects of our lives. Our default position is that continuing sin is a natural and common failing, an unchangeable result of the fall of Adam and Eve, a weakness that is both predictable and expected even among the most sincere Christian believers.

> We have convinced ourselves of our inability, even with God's assisting grace, to give God total control of all aspects of our lives.

The story of David and Goliath is one of good overcoming evil. But in keeping with much theology today, the pathetic fact among Christians is that many of us relate best to another story, the one about Saul and Goliath. Goliath, an intimidating giant of a man, had challenged the Israelites to a duel that he expected to win handily. Instead of putting their trust and confidence in the God who could give them victory, Israel capitulated to the belief system of Goliath. Saul was partly to blame for this poor thinking. The Bible says, "When Saul and all Israel heard these words of the Philistine, they were dismayed and greatly afraid" (1 Sam. 17:11). They had come to the conclusion that winning a conclusive battle against Goliath was impossible. Likewise, God's people today tend to accept sin as the sad necessity in their lives.

The truth of the matter is that when we accept victory as impossible, failure is inevitable—and what is inevitable is predictable. And so, "we sin in word, thought and deed every day." Numerous books declare some limited kind of victory in Christ through grace, but a victory that offers only a slight hope for much spiritual gain in this life. It is a partial victory at best. Goliath is just too big. The tragedy is that we have made spiritual defeat inevitable and almost acceptable. We claim a theoretical victory in Christ while doubting the full meaningfulness of this victory for our daily Christian lives.

This is an awkward discrepancy that we have swallowed. It is what Dallas Willard calls the "disjunction" between faith and life. We should be troubled over this and asking questions like these. Do we think that God gives nothing that really influences our very characters? Can we really believe that God would establish a plan for his children that quietly bypasses the awesome needs of present human life? Why is today's church so weak? Could it be because Christians for the most part are almost indistinguishable from the rest of the world?

These are very important questions. Willard's response to them is astounding to today's Christian culture. He writes, "Should we not at least consider the possibility that this poor result is not in spite of what we teach and how we teach, but precisely because of it?... Once we understand the disconnection between the current message and ordinary life, the failures...at least make a certain sense.... The current gospel...becomes 'a gospel of sin management' (forgiveness is all that matters). Transformation of life and character is no part of the redemptive message."[3] Is this acceptable? Is this all there is? We need holiness to shine again!

Charles Schulz, in one of his famous Peanuts cartoons, shows Pig Pen and Schroeder playing together in the dirt with their toy trucks. Pig Pen says, "I think it's time to go home and take a shower." Schroeder responds with interest, saying, "Going to get all cleaned up, eh, Pig-Pen?" "Well," says Pig-Pen, "I've learned never to expect too much from a shower. I have to be satisfied if it just settles the dust."

Must we be "Pig-Pen" Christians with our sins forgiven while more sin always collects for the next shower time? Or are we like the little fellow who was being scrubbed by a mother who insisted on getting him clean? He cried, "Mommy, that hurts!" "I've got to get you clean," she explained. To which he replied, "Couldn't you just dust me?" So many of us think that God will be satisfied with--maybe is only capable of--a temporary dusting of our sinful lives.

There is a remarkable book by Thomas Upham that dates back to 1858. It records the life and testimony of a great Christian saint of the 1400s named Madame Catharine Adorna. Upham, commenting on the fact of her saintliness, says, "Many have a feeble hope of heaven, as of something dimly in the distance; but small is the number of those (and she was one of this small number) who can speak of an inward heaven and of present victory."[4] He urges that we read more than the numerous memoirs of people who had low visions of what is possible in spiritual attainment. We must not be left with the impression that no better state of things is to be expected or even sought in this present life.

If not for the date, we might think that Upham is speaking of the twenty-first century church when he says, "And whatever may be the cause, it must be admitted as a general statement that the expectations of the church at the present time, in relation to present sanctification and the peace attendant upon such sanctification, are very low. And what is still more afflicting, the feebleness of her efforts, as would naturally be expected, seems to correspond to the humble nature of her expectations."[5]

God refuses to lower the expectation level! God's intent is no less than our transformation into the image of Jesus Christ. This high-level intent should not oppress or depress us frail humans. God knows what we cannot do for ourselves, but we should focus on what we need and what can be done for us. God believes in us—and his cleansing grace is more than sufficient.

Nate, feeling the deep leading of God in his life to take on a new challenge, resigned his very successful tenure as principal of a local high school to get involved in an innovative endeavor called "The Crossing" (an alternative program for high school students who have been expelled from the public school for severe infractions and failures). This program actually seeks these kids out, encouraging them to finish with their studies, requiring high grades to pass a subject. Teachers spend quality time with all students. The results are proving that when someone gives personal attention to a student's need, and refuses to lower the expectations to accommodate bad behavior but actually raises the expectations, there is the God-given human spirit that responds.

Is it possible that, if we could change the constant drumbeat for the inevitability of sin and begin declaring the great intent and ability of God, Christians would begin to rise to a greater hope of spiritual attainment and life practice? We must stop giving in to the voice of defeat and listen to the Apostle Paul: "O, wretched man that I am, who shall deliver me from the body of this death?" The answer? "But thanks be to God, who gives us the victory through our Lord Jesus

Christ" (1 Cor. 15:57). This voice of high hope echoes throughout the Bible and is being carried into our times by the Spirit.

The Way of Holiness Is Possible

One of the great tragedies of our day is that we have made sin bigger than God in our thinking. We have made it both omnipotent and omnipresent, thinking that it is inevitable in our lives. Sadly, many Christians have accepted this kind of reductionist thinking. They are like the fish that was the subject of a scientific experiment.

A fish was placed in a sizeable fish tank with full access to the food-rich tank. After a time, the researchers removed all food and put a glass wall down the middle of the tank. Letting the fish get very hungry, they then placed food on the opposite side of the glass from where the fish was. The fish naturally went after the food, but was immediately brought to a sudden halt when slamming against the invisible glass. The fish tried again and again, only to be rebuffed every time by the glass. Finally, it went back to a corner of the tank and just floated there. Then came the point of the experiment. The researchers removed the dividing glass and put in more food, but the fish just stayed in the corner. The food was moved closer to the fish, but the fish just stayed in its corner, convinced that food was still impossible to reach. Death became inevitable.

Is this the sad scene in today's church? Christ has come. The dividing wall between sinful humans and God has been removed. The riches of God's redeeming and transforming grace have been poured out and are within reach. And yet people have just quit trying to eat and mature spiritually because they have become convinced that they cannot have that for which their hearts hunger. To such deprived believers we say this. Don't quit reaching! Don't quit hoping! Satan wants us to believe that the glass wall is still there as the great impossible in your life. Make another turn. Try one more time. God has removed the partition!

Barack Obama entered into his first term of office as president of the United States on the theme "Yes, we can!" We contend that, when it comes to the sin problem, we need to alter that phrase by changing one word, and then placing God back into the highest of all offices on the theme, "Yes, God can!"

The Apostle Paul raises this possibility to a new level, saying, "We have been buried with Him through baptism into death, in order that as Christ was raised from the dead through the glory of the Father, so we too might walk in newness of life. For if we have become united with Him in the likeness of His death, certainly we shall also be united with him in a resurrection like his, knowing this, that our old self was crucified with Him, that our body of sin might be done away with, that we should no longer be slaves to sin.... Even so, consider yourselves to be dead to sin, but alive to God in Christ Jesus" (Rom. 6:4-6, 11).

The shift from death to life is the path to Christian holiness. We are to be more than forgiven of past sin. We are to be made new creatures in Christ, the forgiven who are actively walking on the road of holiness, now alive to God in Christ Jesus. This incredible new life provided by God's grace had to be what John the Baptist was feeling when he saw Jesus coming to him that dramatic day by the Jordan River. Seeing Jesus, John exclaimed what ought to be our Christian mantra message: "Behold, the Lamb of God who takes away the sin of the world!" (Jn. 1:29). YES, GOD CAN!

John believed because of what he knew
Jesus could do *positionally*

This was God incarnate! The magnitude of this truth gripped John, causing him to exclaim, "He who is coming after me is mightier than I.... He will baptize you with the Holy Spirit and fire" (Matt. 3:11). He knew that Jesus had incredible power at his disposal positionally, that is, because of who he was. His unique position with God makes possible our repositioning before God and our transformation by God's grace.

John believed because of what he knew
Jesus could do *provisionally*

It had to be an incredibly emotional moment in John's life when he looked up and "saw Jesus coming toward him." Stunned by who he was, John declared, "Behold, the Lamb of God who takes away the sin of the world!" Every Jew who heard him that day understood the concept of "the lamb of God," but to have John associate this grand concept with Jesus and, more than that, emphasize "who takes away the sin of the world," was nothing short of revolutionary. It was either bold truth or shocking blasphemy. Who Jesus is in relation to God meant that what Jesus could provide for us is fully adequate for our deepest needs.

John, as a prophet of God, got hold of the extent of Christ's provision for the sinful condition of humans. The greatest news (the gospel) is that Christ came to deal fully with the problem of sin. This highlights the meaning of Isaiah 53:4-6: "Surely he took up our infirmities.... He was pierced for our transgressions, he was crushed for our iniquities; the punishment that brought us peace was upon him, and by his wounds we are healed." Jesus came to make us like himself, intending a genuine deliverance from all sin.

There is no doubt that believing in the great deliverance possible by God through the Spirit of Jesus is sometimes difficult in this sin-drenched world. I (Barry) have strolled around the outer decks of large cruise ships in many of the seas of the world. I once sailed with my wife up the amazing Nile River through the desert of Egypt and toward the mountains of Ethiopia. For a few amazing minutes one sunny day I even got to pilot the "Black Pearl," a (tourist) pirate ship positioned off the eastern shore of Honduras. Often in my travels I found myself gazing across the great blue-green expanse of waters, pondering my good fortune. I have realized again how insignificant I am, a mere speck in the great surging expanse of it all. The sheer grace, the immeasurable grace of God is surely the dominant reality of our world and of our walk with God. Who can say that this grace is inadequate for our spiritual needs?

Reversing the "Great Impossible"

God wants to reverse the "great impossible" that has dominated our vision and determined our theology for too long. God wants us to know and pursue holiness as a doctrine to be believed, an experience to be received, a message to be declared, and a way of life to be demonstrated before a hungry world.[6]

A way of life to be demonstrated—this is where the rubber meets the road. If holiness is to mean anything, this is where it must shine or it is a sham. Does holiness stand a chance under the twists and turns of life? We say, "Yes!" True holiness poured into our hearts works, not in our power but by the power of God in us. The Apostle Paul staked the integrity of his ministry on this fact, saying to any Christian, anywhere, anytime, under any circumstance: "No testing has overtaken you that is not common to everyone. God is faithful, and he will not let you be tested beyond your strength, but with the testing he will also provide the way out so that you may be able to endure it" (1 Cor. 10:13). You can go through the fire and it will not destroy you. You can go through the deep waters and manage to survive. How? By being bathed in the life-changing beauty of God's grace.

This holiness is not something *out of* this world. It is holiness *in* this world. We are not talking about strange saintly figures lost in unreality with halos over their heads, but normal human beings dealing with all the nitty-gritty issues of life. Sin is not "normal" in God's world. The grace-full colors of God are ready and able to redesign discolored lives in real time and in real circumstances—making human beings more fully human as God made us originally, "crowned with glory and honor" (Ps. 8:5). Holiness does not result in artificial super Christians, but in humble believers who have taken hold of God's promise. What promise? That God will keep his children each moment of every day, showering them with divine holiness and making them witnesses to God's transforming power.

> Holiness does not result in artificial super Christians, but in humble believers who have taken hold of God's promise of transforming grace.

We are pleased to share six particular places where divine grace can deliver and commission believers in today's churches.

Under Pressure

One of the more impactful books we have ever read was written by Harry Jessop in 1941. He was a Christian evangelist, teacher, and author who also served as president of a small Bible college. The book's title, *I Met A Man with a Shining Face*, is as fascinating as the content. Jessop had encountered a young man deeply committed to the Christian faith and only deepened in his faith by the persecution he faced. This is the kind of testimony that can be a Christian's greatest witness to the world. The idea of a shining face speaks of divine presence as reported in the Old Testament and of the Holy Spirit as presented in the New. God longs to shine the divine glory on his people. We read: "The Lord bless you and keep you; the Lord make his face to shine upon you, and be gracious to you; the Lord lift up his countenance upon you, and give you peace" (Nu. 6:23-26).

One of the standouts of a Spirit-filled life was Stephen. He was chosen for vital ministry at a critical time in the church because he was "a man full of faith and of the Holy Spirit" (Acts 6:5). When facing the wrath of his accusers, Luke records that "all who sat in the council looked intently at him, and they saw that his face was like the face of an angel" (Acts 6:15). It had to do with a holy presence filling a hungry soul and spilling over to touch those nearby. Stephen left an unforgettable testimony to the possibility of the presence and power of the Holy Spirit in a Christian's life under pressure.

Jesus insisted that this presence would be the Holy Spirit (Jn. 14-16) with us today. "I tell you the truth: it is to your advantage that I go away, for if I do not go away, the Advocate will not come to you; but if I go, I will send him to you" (Jn. 16:7). The Spirit is the "game changer" under pressure, reversing the "great impossible" of our lives. What comes out of our lives under pressure? Is it sweet or bitter? Is it pure or contaminated? Is it Christ-like or full of self? Pray that God will color us holy by filling us with living water from on high.

Pressure is what has to be put on any fruit to get out the juice. That may be the reason God often allows pressure in our lives. We may not like it, but God uses negative circumstances as a witness to a world that needs to see the difference in someone who is going through illness, reversals, or a difficult relationship. Do you know the presence of the Holy Spirit in all his purity and healing comfort? Only with that presence can we leave a shining witness in the world.

Through Darkness

We and so many others have dealt with cancer personally or with a parent or spouse. We have known the pain that comes from loss of loved ones. Can holiness shine in such darkness? Luke, in writing the book of Acts, says it again and again--"Yes, it can!" This is where it really shines. We've seen it. We know it. We've heard it in the darkest prisons. We've seen it in the crashing storms. We were there. We know!

Not long ago a crowd gathered to pay respect for the memory of someone who had lived joyously and sincerely before the Lord for many years. One could not help but appreciate and applaud the un-sullied testimony of Wilfred, one of God's true saints. Alice and Wilfred had not lived holiness in a vacuum. They knew what suffering was. They had raised two boys and a girl and one day had to stand at the graveside of their oldest son who had been killed in a tractor accident. Later they had to stand at another graveside as they buried their only daughter. The grief was overwhelming, but hope remained strong. Even in their suffering, they kept radiating the beauty of God's holiness, not barely, but gloriously. When the news was given to Alice about her son's tragic accident, she was heard to say, "I wonder what lessons God will teach me through this?"

The glow of God's comforting and sustaining presence was then seen in that respectful crowd as Wilfred buried his beloved wife. True holiness is never lived in a vacuum. It does not make one "safe" from the sometimes harsh realities of life. God's saints go through pain and feel pain deeply, probably more deeply than anyone else because they love so deeply. Still, they face pain differently. Their faces have been full toward God and they are able lift their heads and keep looking up into that gracious face. In their pain, rather than drawing attention to their grief, they draw full attention to God's grace. That is what Luke saw as he researched the lives of those who would fill the stories in his Gospel. Holiness was—and is--alive and well!

The strength of holiness is in the word "wait" as explained in Isaiah 40:31. Isaiah notes that "even youths will faint and be weary, and the young will fall exhausted" (40:30). Then he declares, "but those who wait for the Lord shall renew their strength, they shall mount up with wings like eagles, they shall run and not be weary, they shall walk and not faint" (40:31). The word "wait" is a Hebrew word that means "to bind with by twisting." It carries the idea of being "intertwined with," as in a rope's construction. In other words, those who bind themselves in this God-rope or *intertwine* themselves with the Lord "shall renew their strength, they shall mount up with wings like eagles, they shall run and not be weary, they shall walk and not faint."

This rope is a picture of holiness, and it will hold as one gropes in the darkness of life's difficulties. We may pass through deep waters and have to walk through fire, but the promise of Isaiah 43:1-2 holds true for all who are full face toward God: "But now thus says the Lord, he who created you, O Jacob, he who formed you, O Israel: Do not fear, for I have redeemed you; I have called you by name, you are mine. When you pass through the waters, I will be with you; and through the rivers, they shall not overwhelm you; when you walk through fire you shall not be burned, and the flame shall not consume you.

With Relationships

Missionaries and pastors have been known to say half seriously, "I could enjoy doing this work if it weren't for people." Some have thought it would be nice to serve on an uninhabited island. Without doubt, relationships are the greatest test grounds for holiness. It is interesting that the writer to the Hebrews speaks of holiness in the same breath as keeping peace: "Pursue peace with everyone, and the holiness without which no one will see the Lord" (Heb. 12:14).

Early World Gospel Mission missionaries in China were noted for their unity. Those who knew most intimately the WGM group in China and their relations each to the other were "most deeply impressed with the harmony that has always prevailed in the group. The secret lies in waiting before the Lord. They were never too pressed with daily tasks to tarry until the will of the Holy Spirit was made evident upon plans and policies. This harmonious unity goes far to explain the teamwork and success achieved. The Holy Spirit had right of way."[7] Therefore, God's children were marked with the glowing grace of God's great heart.

All too many marriages, homes, and work relationships have fallen apart because of stubborn, sinful self-centeredness. Where unholy attitudes and actions are allowed to rule, they only divide. We are witnessing the high probability of breakdown and the nigh impossibility of keeping something together when the unsanctified self is active. Paul says, "And this is my prayer, that your love may overflow more and more with knowledge and full insight to help you to determine what is best, so that in the day of Christ you may be pure [sincere] and blameless (Phil. 1:9-10). The greatest hope for holy matrimony is a holy heart. The same is true with any human relationship.

Not until the 1870s would two men, Pasteur and Lister, finally convince the medical world of the need for basic hygiene in surgery. Thousands of lives had been lost because the medical world had not realized the importance of simple hygiene. Why do we keep going down the same road no matter the death rate? Why will we not allow heart cleansing before we begin to practice housekeeping? For centuries now, God has been trying to convince the human race of the importance of holiness—a clean heart. How many more relationships will have to fall apart before we finally get it? In fact, some do get it but are not prepared to surrender a stubborn and selfish will.

> We do not need more holiness talk. We need more holiness walk!

We do not need more holiness talk. We need more holiness walk. We are sick of the hypocrisy that has prevailed in too many Christian settings. The cure is not in denigrating hypocrites but in living true holiness. When true holiness of heart and life seep into our homes, churches, mission agencies, Christian organizations and Christian institutions, healthy relationships will come alive and thrive—even in the face of differences. Any of us can be a health bringer if we will just let God "color me beautiful."

Over Physical Appetites

One of the greatest problems we face in society today is the lack of control over physical appetites. Television and the internet have increased the problem, making sin at this level much more appealing and accessible. Although this especially involves sexual sins, it also includes obesity and the drive to satisfy an insatiable thirst for more and more pleasure and "stuff." If ever there were the need for holiness, it is here.

Many new converts now come into Christian experience with horrific baggage and incredible addictions—sex, alcohol, food, phones, and buying addictions. Is holiness possible here? There is a progression of important questions that we need to ask in relation to sin and God's power to deliver. Can God deliver from *one* sin? Can God deliver from *any* sin? Can God deliver from *all* sin? To all of these questions we answer, "Yes, God can!"

Steve suffered with obesity. It affected his energy level, his spirit, and his ministry. He had tried different kinds of diet programs only to fail again and again. But now, 140 pounds lighter and maintaining, Steve loves to tell what God did. It took some people to speak to him about the abuse he was bringing to his body—which they pointed out was the temple of the Holy Spirit. God sweetly convicted him and he humbly listened. Seeing himself as body, soul, and spirit, and that his addiction to food affected the whole, he sought God's help and, with the guidance of a medical nutritionist, began a change of lifestyle. Anyone will tell you, Steve is a different man now—in body, soul, and spirit.

Wholeness requires a radical change of lifestyle to which many are not willing to submit. Yes, holiness includes a comprehensive lifestyle, but all that some people want is a momentary fix. We humans like the healing part but not the "go and sin no more" part. Unfortunately, one is not available without the other. However, and we praise God for this, anyone can know and do both!

The Word of God is loaded with hope and possibility. Everything God does in this world is toward the reversal of all that the fall of humanity has brought into this world. Recall the question of Jesus to the paralytic: "Do you want to be made well?" (literally, "whole"). Recall what Paul announced to the Corinthians: "So if anyone is in

Christ, there is a new creation: everything old has passed away; see, everything has become new!" (2 Cor. 5:17). These words should cause us to dance with the paralytics and cripples who were made completely whole by Jesus. Says Jesus, come dance with me. The colors of new creation are bright and beautiful!

In the Marketplace

The Bible makes it very clear-- "You shall love the Lord your God with all your heart, and with all your soul, and with all your strength, and with all your mind" and you shall love "your neighbor as yourself" (Lk. 10:27). There are two words in Scripture that travel together like two rails that make one track. Those words are "holiness" and "righteousness." True to the original meaning, the word "righteous" in Spanish Bibles is translated *justicia* which means justice—having to do with doing what is right and just toward others. We cannot speak of the holiness of God without speaking of the righteousness of God. We might speak of holiness as the *heart* of God and righteousness as the *hands* of God. Likewise, our *being* and *doing* both must reflect holiness or neither has integrity.

In the believer's life, holiness without righteousness becomes hard, cold, exacting, legalistic, critical, and selfish. On the other hand, righteousness without holiness is as filthy rags. Its tendency is to become self-important, doing good works to impress God and others. It leads to social action without salvation. If we are to survive and thrive as followers of Jesus Christ, we must seek holiness and do righteousness. Otherwise, we will get off track and derail.

John Wesley was one who rode well these two rails of holiness and righteousness and called other believers to do the same. During his long ministry and even as he looked back on the movement at the end of his life, his great concern was the tendency among "Methodists" to have zeal without knowledge. In keeping with our metaphor, he feared that if they continued to ride the one rail without the other they would derail. To lack or be slack in either is to kill the other. To grow and mature in either is to quicken the other.

A profound moment in my (Hubert) life was on a visit to Kenya several years ago. Dr. Phil Renfroe had asked for permission to be my chauffer back to Nairobi. Without my knowing it, there was an ulterior motive in his request. He wanted to impact my life with someone who had impacted his. We would be having lunch with a Dennis Tongoi who is now the director of the Anglican Church in Eastern Africa. This Kenyan had spoken into Phil's life great spiritual truths—leading him into the true meaning of righteousness and justice. Phil became a champion for "wholistic community transformation." It was in this context that I began to really understand Zacharias' words concerning Jesus, and now they struck me with incredible force: "to grant us that we, being rescued from the hands of our enemies, might serve him without fear, *in holiness and righteousness* before him all our days" (Lu. 1:73-75, emphasis added).

I (Barry) wrote "Let's Get On the Train!" for the July 3, 1977, issue of *Vital Christianity*, then the national periodical of the Church of God (Anderson). In this article I recalled being literally pushed by a moving traffic jam of hurrying humans into a commuter train in Tokyo, Japan. I used that experience to bring perspective on our whole planet that is now jammed with humans who have growing needs and shrinking resources. I said: "Our Lord keeps sending us to the despairing poor with words of love and deeds of sacrificial caring. He keeps urging us into the marketplace where the pains of life are inflicted and suffered. How much better if God would leave us in peace inside our air-conditioned churches where there is no rush for seats! But it just isn't that way. Apparently there is no other way to heaven except by responsible relatedness to our many brothers and sisters who are caught in the whirl of things. So let's get on the train!"

On the Way

Someone was asked what war is like. The simple answer was, "90% boredom and 10% sheer terror." In many ways, life is like that. The phrase "the way of holiness" is classic because it is not merely lifting up some great emotional experience people may want to have. It is not speaking only of exciting experiences with which people may fill their lives. It is also "the way." It is a distinctive life, all of it, all the way.

The word "walk" is used in Scripture to depict a godly person's daily, steady, ongoing, and living relationship with God. Hezekiah caught the essence of this walk when he called spoke of "faithfulness with a whole heart" (2 Kings 20:3). This is holiness every day along the way. Holiness is not merely spiritual "hype." It does not leave us out of breath trying to keep up with God—trying to be holy by our own accelerated momentum. Holiness, by contrast, is more the quiet presence of God taking our hand and walking with us.

Anne Marie, the daughter of Congolese missionaries, speaks of her love of the idea behind an expression she often heard as a child: *malembe malembe.* Carrying it as her mantra, Anne says that literally it means "slowly, slowly." But as with most Lingala phrases, these words are packed full of nuanced meaning. They imply little steps, focusing on what matters and not being overwhelmed with the big picture, remaining faithful despite the long road. It is also a hopeful phrase in that it connotes realization of a vision, but only with slow, faithful, step by step walking."[8] The colors of God's presence must be seen and reflected in the drab of every day.

The idea of "radical Christianity" is being marketed today as discipleship involving extreme commitments and causes. But unless the *malembe malembe* is in our walk with God, our running without any walking and resting will go up like a blaze fueled by gasoline and just as quickly die. Our hearts must be driven by a different kind of fuel— a fire fueled by the holy glory of God poured into our hearts slowly, deeply, daily. This is a different kind of "radical Christianity"[9] than the hype of emotions for dramatic Christian service. This is the radical Christianity of the book of Acts that affected the early disciples with a Holy Spirit who inspired them. This was the power of their witness (Acts 1:8), a power that caused others down through history to step apart from the dominating drag of traditional religion. We can know the holiness of God in every area and moment of our lives. In Christ this can be an actual reality.

I (Barry) was nine years old when a great storm hit northeast Ohio on the Thanksgiving weekend of 1950. A total of twenty-nine inches of snow buried the area, with high winds creating drifts as much as ten feet deep. The paralysis kept many people isolated in their homes for nearly a week. The National Guard was called to assist in road clearing. I remember Dad and me digging a trench from our house down the middle of Beach Lane to reach Baldwin's Market near the entrance to the amusement park, a distance of two blocks. It was both frightening and fascinating, clearly inconvenient and truly inspiring for a young boy. I could imagine that under the snow all the ugly things on the roads and in the ditches were now cleansed and gone. The world had been reborn. While such mass redemption was only in my imagination, in Christ it can be an actual reality!

We say it as strongly as we can. Such a vision of the world reborn is not to be limited to the imagination of a little boy or to a few "saints" living behind monastery walls. This grand possibility can produce a new generation like the one of John Wesley and the people first called "Methodists." They believed in the vast riches of God's transforming grace and turned their world upside down with a holiness fire that God set burning in their hearts.

Paul wrote of the role of the Spirit of God in our lives and stressed the pentecostal theme of first fruits. We who have believed in God through Jesus Christ "were marked with the promised Holy Spirit; this is the pledge of our inheritance toward redemption as God's own people, to the praise of his glory" (Eph. 1:13-14). Again: "But it is God who establishes us with you in Christ and has anointed us by putting his seal on us and giving us his Spirit in our hearts as a first install-ment" (2 Cor. 1:21-22). We who are born of the Spirit are enabled to live like the Spirit to the praise of God's shining glory.

> We who are born of the Spirit are enabled to live like the Spirit to the praise of God's shining glory.

There it is, the great word spoken to our impoverished spiritual lives. The Spirit of God has come as the first installment of the full inheritance to be received by us. Eventually that inheritance will come to include a bodily resurrection and the full new creation that God has promised. Indeed, one day "the creation itself will be set free from its bondage to decay and will obtain the freedom of the glory of the children of God" (Rom. 8:21). That will be then. What about now? How are Christians to wait for the full arrival of God's promises? We are to wait in full expectation. We are to settle in the meantime for nothing less than all that God has for us. We are to pray to God, "color me ho-ly!"

Don't Miss Out

Holiness will not let us stay in the little world of our own domain. It brings divine restoration followed by vital disciplines and intentional discipleship—involving us in the things that matter most to God. Many people, even Christians, would rather not give up their own wants and lifestyles. Tragically, like Judas the betrayer, they do not have a clue as to what they are missing. Judas missed out on the joy of Jesus' resurrection, the hope of the ascension, the coming of the Holy Spirit, and the life of the church and its dramatic advancement of the God's kingdom. He never saw the change in Peter, James and John, along with the incredible change in the other disciples. He nev-er met Stephen, Paul, Luke, Timothy, Priscilla and so many others whose lives were dipped in the amazing colors of God's holiness. He missed out on it all. Don't you miss out!

Here is the music of the ages. Heaven will resound with this sound and be lighted by the colorful flashes of this truth. The voices of those who know the deep meaning of the words will sing this throughout eternity: "Worthy is the Lamb that was slaughtered to receive power and wealth and wisdom and might and honor and glory and blessing!" (Rev. 5:12). Be hungry for God's loving colors to be painted on the canvas of your heart and life. Will you join us in the prayer below for the church as a whole? Will you personalize it and make it yours? God is wanting to answer your prayer. The divine heart shines in these verses:

> I pray that the God of our Lord Jesus Christ, the Father of glory, may give you a spirit of wisdom and revelation as you come to know him, so that, with the eyes of your heart enlightened, you may know what is the hope to which he has called you, what are the riches of his glorious inheritance among the saints, and what is the immeasurable greatness of his power for us who believe, according to the working of his great power.... God, who is rich in mercy, out of the great love with which he loved us even when we were dead through our trespasses, made us alive together with Christ (by grace you are saved) and raised us up with him and seated us with him in the heavenly places in Christ Jesus.... I pray that, according to the riches of his glory, he may grant that you may be streng-thened in your inner being with power through his Spirit, and that Christ may dwell in your hearts through faith, as you are being rooted and grounded in love. I pray that you may have the power to comprehend, with all the saints, what is the breadth and length and height and depth, and to know the love of Christ that surpasses knowledge, so that you may be filled with all the fullness of God. Now to him who by the power at work within us is able to accomplish abundantly far more than all we can ask or imagine, to him be glory in the church and in Christ Jesus to all generations, forever and ever. Amen (Eph. 1:17-20; 2:4-6; 3:14-20).

To this classic biblical prayer we add this:

> Abba, Father, please cleanse the canvas of our hearts, removing the dark colors of sin and self that cloud our lives, and sanctify us with the brightness of your pure colors so that our lives might glow with a testimony of your presence and beauty, that all who come in contact with us might taste and see that it is good and give you glory for lives lived in your holiness and with your righteous-ness. Amen!

Notes

[1] Leon R. Kass, "The Wisdom of Repugance," essay in *The New Republic*, June 2, 1997. 17-26.

[2] N. T. Wright, *After You Believe: Why Character Matters* (HarperCollins, 2010), 27.

[3] Dallas Williard, *The Divine Conspiracy: Rediscovering Our Hidden Life in God* (HarperCollins Publishers, New York, NY, 1998), 39, 38.

[4] Thomas C. Upham, *Life of Madame Catharine Adorna* (republished by Forgotten Books, 2012), 16.

[5] Ibid, 14-15.

[6] This line of thought it taken from the Constitution of World Gospel Mission.

[7] Burnis Bushong, *Reaching the Unreached Now: A Brief History of World Gospel Mission* (World Gospel Mission, 1995), 12.

[8] Email from Anne Marie Thomason, February 27, 2013.

[9] See Barry L. Callen, *Radical Christianity: The Believers Church Tradition in Christianity's History and Future* (Evangel Publishing House, 1999).

CPSIA information can be obtained
at www.ICGtesting.com
Printed in the USA
FFOW04n0814011214
9101FF